THE FANS
LOVE STORY

FROM ONE
DIRTY DANCING FAN
TO ANOTHER,

LET'S "DIRTY DANCE"
THROUGH LIFE &
SPREAD THE LOVE !

BEST WISHES,

SUE

THE FANS' LOVE STORY

How The Movie
'DIRTY DANCING'
Captured The
Hearts Of Millions!

Sue Tabashnik

Outskirts Press, Inc.
Denver, Colorado

THE FANS' LOVE STORY
How The Movie '*DIRTY DANCING*' Captured The Hearts Of Millions!
All Rights Reserved.
Copyright © 2010 Sue Tabashnik
v4.0

COPYRIGHT PERMISSIONS
I gratefully thank these sources for giving permission to use their material.

1. Copyright © 2008 *Broadwayfanclub.com*. "Dirty Dancing: A Legendary Story on National Tour." The Broadway League. August 2008 Newsletter.
2. Copyright © 2009 *Jewish Journal*. "'Dirty Dancing' Comes Alive on Stage." Rick Schultz. May 20, 2009.
3. Copyright © 2008 *Chicago Tribune*. "'Dirty Dancing' creator keeps the legend alive." Sid Smith. September 28, 2008.
4. Copyright © 2005 *Globe Newspaper Company*. "Stay'in Alive." Mark Shanahan. *The Boston Globe*. September 29, 2005.
5. Copyright © 1988 *ABC. Barbara Walters Special Interview*.
6. Copyright © 2006 *Whatsonstage.com*. "Photos: Swayze & Sweeney Ready to Play in Dolls." Terri Paddock. June 5, 2006.
7. Copyright © 2008 *FemaleFirst.co.uk*. "Miranda Garrison talks Dirty Dancing." September 2, 2008.
8. Copyright © 2006 *Guardian News & Media*. "Patrick Swayze on 'Dirty Dancing.'" *Telegraph.co.uk*. September 23, 2006.
9. Copyright © 1988 *Times Herald-Record*. "Film thrills Horner." August 18, 1987.
10. Copyright © "Biographical Sketch—Jackie Horner." Jackie Horner.
11. Copyright © 2006 *Guardian News & Media*. "There's a secret dancer inside us all." Veronica Lee. *Telegraph.co.uk*. September 26, 2006.
12. Copyright © 2009 *Mountain Lake Hotel. Mountainlakehotel.com*.
13. Copyright © 2008 *Chicago Tribune*. "Swayze feels at home in Chicago." Robert K. Elder. November 18, 2009.
14. Copyright © 1988 *Detroit Free Press*. "Movie makes her do the mambo, not the munch-o." Neal Rubin. January 7, 1988.
15. Copyright © 2003 *Arts Houston Magazine*. "One Last Dance." Patrick Swayze. April 2003.

Outskirts Press, Inc.
http://www.outskirtspress.com

ISBN: 978-1-4327-5110-4

Outskirts Press and the "OP" logo are trademarks belonging to Outskirts Press, Inc.
PRINTED IN THE UNITED STATES OF AMERICA

To Mr. Patrick Swayze—who plays a hero in *Dirty Dancing* and who has been and will always be a hero in real life to me and to millions of people all over the world.

I have special gratitude to you for being such an inspiration— for how you lived your life, full of zest—and for the messages that you communicated by your artistry, actions, and words: to follow dreams, to partake in the arts, to "rock 'n roll," and "spread the love." I really appreciate the devotion that you showed to your fans for years. You and Ms. Lisa Niemi have been an amazing example of dedication and love to the arts, and most important, dedication and love to each other and your families.

Thank you from the bottom of my heart for your continual "re-discovery of innocence" and for inspiring the same in me.

Your battle with pancreatic cancer counted and will never be forgotten. We will carry on the fight.

You have been and always will be a big, big bright light in my life that is an anchor for decency, humanness, spirit, and compassion.

Contents

INTRODUCTION

When I first started writing an article about *Dirty Dancing* in 2006, I never dreamed that it would turn into a book. I just knew that the movie had deeply resonated with me and that the 20th anniversary of the movie was coming up in 2007. I wanted to shout out to the world about this unbelievably wonderful movie, to honor this movie and the people who made it. Also, perhaps there was a bit of the social worker in me that wanted to explore the wonderful phenomenon of this 1987 movie. Why was *Dirty Dancing* still capturing, with no sign of slowing down, the hearts of people all over the world—including mine? Furthermore, maybe in my search, I would validate my attachment to the movie.

After completing the article, I made the jump into writing the book. I was rather naive about what it takes to write and publish a book. I must say that I ran into many roadblocks regarding writing an independent book focused on a movie. During this time period, unexpected and very stressful events occurred, as five important people in my life had life-threatening health crises. Two of these key people died within three weeks of each other—Ms. Lee Santiwan, my mentor, and Mr. Patrick Swayze. (In terms of time frame, just six days before Mr. Swayze passed, this manuscript was accepted for publishing.)

In the past two years or so, I persisted in completing the book with support and encouragement from many, many people. I derived a great deal of inspiration from Mr. Patrick Swayze—by his amazing spirit, tenacity, and dignity in his battle against pancreatic cancer—and from Ms. Lee Santiwan—by her wisdom, amazing support, and lesson in dealing with illness with dignity. I will be forever grateful to both of them.

With all of that said, I would not trade this journey for the world. I met amazing people, ages seventeen to eighty-three—from four continents and all different walks of life—who were also totally enthralled with the movie and were open in sharing their connections to the movie. Each person had his or her own unique alliance to the movie, along with sharing in some universal linkages. By hearing each person's journey, I satisfied my desire to explore the *Dirty Dancing* phenomenon in the world and within me, and came away with a renewed sense of faith in the spirit of man-womankind.

In transitioning from the article to the book, my first step was creating an online survey that was posted on the Internet by Mrs. Margaret Howden in November 2007, from which I received 186 responses by August 2008. I interviewed twenty-two people in-person, by telephone, or via e-mail—or by some combination of these modalities. I chose fifteen of the twenty-two fan interviewees from the people who answered the survey and seven via other ways—from referrals and known *Dirty Dancing* fans.

I journeyed to Mountain Lake Hotel in Pembroke, Virginia—one of the two major film locations—in January 2009, and had the amazing experience of being there first-hand to see, feel, and learn about this *Dirty Dancing* historical site. I had the absolute good fortune to have Mr. H. M. "Buzz" Scanland Jr., General Manager—who was present during the filming of the movie—show me around and impart to me a wealth of information, verbal and written (including access to archives on the movie). I then had the wonderful opportunity to telephone interview two other people who were present during the filming—Mr. Mike Porterfield, Executive Chef at Mountain Lake Hotel, and Mr. Gary Wilson, Head of Security at Rumbling Bald Resort, the film location for the golf course scene.

I had the absolute pleasure to correspond by writing and telephone with Ms. Jackie Horner. She served as a consultant to the filmmakers (see "special thanks to Jackie Horner" on the screen credits) as she was the dance pro at Grossinger's in the Catskills from 1954 to 1986. She has led an amazing, legendary career in the entertainment business and is still going strong. Finally, I had the wonderful, fascinating experience of interviewing Mr. Steve Schwartz by telephone regarding his years as a dancer in the Catskills—including being the dance partner of Ms. Horner at Grossinger's. Ms. Horner refers to Mr. Schwartz as being the person whom the character "Johnny" is based on.

Even with the passing of Mr. Patrick Swayze, I would encourage you to sit back, relax, reminisce, and indulge yourself during this *Dirty Dancing* trip because what a great way to honor a man who loved and lived life to its fullest and did a phenomenal job in portraying the character of Johnny.

One

MY CONNECTION TO *DIRTY DANCING* AND WHY I THINK IT CONTINUES TO GO ON AND ON

"That was the summer of 1987," and I followed my usual weekend passion of going to a movie. Little did I know how much watching this particular movie would change my life. The movie happened to be *Dirty Dancing*. Need I say more? I confess that I was one of "those women" who saw the movie multiple times. Yes, I became a member of the "100 club." At that "time of my life," I had recently gone through a very difficult break-up with the man that I thought was my soul mate. Watching this movie not only provided a very nice escape, but also seemed to impart that all again would be right in the world—that true love could exist against tremendous odds. I came to the conclusion that watching this movie was very soothing, even better than reading self-help books, and in a way just as good as counseling. The story was great, the music was fantastic, and the dancing was powerful. Finally, there was this sizzling, passionate actor/dancer by the name of Mr. Patrick Swayze, who played the lead heartthrob (the "Nobody puts Baby in a corner" guy). I was hooked into becoming a huge fan of Mr. Swayze. The more I watched his work, heard him give interviews, and read about him, the bigger my connection became to him.

After one contact with a fan club in 1987 (I received an autographed picture of Mr. Swayze), the years went by with me still being an avid fan. While searching the Internet in 2000, I struck gold, and found an active fan club—

The Official Patrick Swayze International Fan Club—and big surprise, I joined! I really didn't have any idea what to expect. Was I living out some adolescent fantasy by joining? What the heck! The dues were reasonable, and I would be receiving quarterly magazines and pictures—and hopefully could learn more about Mr. Swayze. After all, I didn't have to tell anybody that I was a member. I had never contemplated contacting a Hollywood star before, and I had certainly never pictured myself belonging to a fan club. Was I now a groupie? I had a picture in my mind of Elvis fans swooning at Graceland and of hysterical women following stars around the country. After mailing in my dues, I had an immediate response from the club president, Mrs. Margaret Howden from Scotland, and felt welcomed into this group. Soon, I could see that this was serious business, and that there were others who had "this thing" for Mr. Swayze. Maybe I wasn't losing my marbles after all.

Actually, as it has turned out, I have enjoyed many different activities through the fan club. I met Mr. Swayze four times—and had the opportunity to hold conversations with him individually and as part of a group. I met him at two dance benefits for the extraordinary dance company Complexions Contemporary Ballet—right here in Detroit—in 2002 and then again in 2004. I also met Mr. Swayze and Ms. Niemi at two film festivals—WorldFest-Houston International Film Festival in 2003 and Nashville Film Festival in 2004—that were showing their magnificent dance movie, *One Last Dance*. Their accessibility to us fans at both of the film festivals was really amazing. Then, in 2005, I had the opportunity to call in a question to Mr. Swayze on *The Big Idea with Donny Deutsch* CNBC television show.

Throughout the years, I have had the good fortune to make some long-lasting, great friendships with some of the other fans in the club. I have also been able to develop my writing skills and use my creativity by writing twelve articles that were published in the fan club magazine. Finally, it has been very special and wonderful to be part of a community supporting someone who was not only enormously talented as an actor, dancer, singer, song writer, producer, and choreographer, but who was also about traditional values, family, a solid work ethic, integrity, spirituality, passion, and activities (such as advocating for the arts, conservation, and cancer research) to make the world a better place. And I need to mention how Mr.

Swayze loved animals, especially Arabian horses, and his support to The Arabian Horse Association.

As mentioned in the Introduction, I started writing this book in 2007, long before Mr. Swayze was diagnosed with cancer. It was absolutely heartbreaking and devastating to find out about Mr. Swayze's Stage IV pancreatic cancer diagnosis. As part of the community supporting him prior to the cancer diagnosis and after the diagnosis, I have always considered it to be a privilege. I was and will continue to be amazed and inspired by him—by his wonderful spirit and heroic battle for life.

I have read Mr. Swayze's guestbook since becoming a fan club member in 2000, and read it more closely and more often following Mr. Swayze's cancer diagnosis. I can tell you that there are thousands and thousands of messages that were sent to him from fans of all ages (five and up) and from all over the world, telling how much they love *Dirty Dancing* and what a special part *Dirty Dancing* has played and will continue to play in their lives.

In addition, *Dirty Dancing* has scored very high in numerous polls and surveys. In February 2008, the *Daily Mail* in the United Kingdom reported that *Dirty Dancing* has the number one most romantic quote ever: Baby saying, "I'm scared of walking out of this room and never feeling for the rest of my whole life the way I feel when I am with you." Also, the *Daily Mail* printed a story on May 6, 2007 that listed *Dirty Dancing* as the number-one movie that women watch. In July 2005, *The Scotsman* ran a story that reported the water lift scene was voted number one as the most favorite scene of all time in a poll answered by almost 1,200 people. In February 2008, per *ananova.com*, an online DVD rental delivery service, *LOVEFILM. com* listed *Dirty Dancing* as the second best feel-good movie. Per an E! Entertainment Television 2007 poll of industry executives and celebrities, *Dirty Dancing* was named as one of the Top Ten Date movies of all time. In 2004, around 200,000 people in the United Kingdom voted out of 100 movies, *Dirty Dancing*, as their favorite movie per ITV. In May 2009, *Dirty Dancing* won as Britain's favorite film in an online poll conducted by the Cinema Advertising Association. Finally, there are three other fun examples of the continuing popularity of *Dirty Dancing* that I just cannot leave out. In a February 21, 2008 survey done by UK Cinema Industry for the "best movie couple," Ms. Grey and Mr. Swayze came in third place. Among female voters, *Dirty Dancing* took second place (lost to *Ghost)* in the best screen kiss poll conducted in the UK by Denplan in honor of the 13th annual National Kissing Day in July 2008. In a 2009 Valentine's Day poll done by HMV, *Ghost* was number one for the best love film, and *Dirty Dancing* placed second.

The stage version of *Dirty Dancing*, written by Ms. Eleanor Bergstein, the writer/co-producer of the movie, has been a brilliant success in Australia (the world premiere was in Sydney in 2004), New Zealand, Germany, and London's West End. In November 2007, the stage show opened in Toronto—with 1.65 million in first-day ticket sales. Next, the production opened in the Netherlands and then in the United States—first stop was Chicago (September 28, 2008), then Boston (February 8, 2009), and finally Los Angeles (April 28, 2009). There is speculation that the next US stop will be Broadway, and by the time that you are reading this book, maybe that will have occurred.

Multiple sources indicate that for about seventeen years, Ms. Bergstein resisted doing the stage play, but then realized that the audience wanted to be there—to be more intensely involved in the experience—and thus she determined that this would be satisfied by a theatrical experience. In an interview "Dirty Dancing: A Legendary Story on National Tour" that Ms. Bergstein gave to The Broadway Fan Club in August 2008, Ms. Bergstein was asked, "What was your starting point when you set out to reconceive this hit movie as a stage production?" Ms. Bergstein answered, "I wanted to find a way to transform it into a new kind of theatrical event . . . I wanted a form that would honor our open-hearted audience . . . And one that might bring into the theatre a new audience that has had its most profound experiences at movies and rock concerts."[1] Rick Schultz in *The Jewish Journal* "'Dirty Dancing' Comes Alive on Stage" on May 20, 2009 wrote, "Bergstein said she waited until 2004 to do a stage adaptation because 'it seemed that the film stood by itself, and I never wanted the audience to feel I was taking advantage of them just to make money.'"[2] Furthermore, Mr. Schultz reported, " . . . despite being two decades old, the movie's continuing popularity suggested to Bergstein that 'people might want to step through the flat screen and have it happen around them, and that meant live theater.'"[2] Finally, Mr. Schultz wrote that Ms. Bergstein said, "Everybody has a secret dancer inside them . . . It's dancing that makes you feel, 'That could be me.'"[2] To sum up, Eleanor Bergstein was asked in the Broadway Fan Club interview—Q: "What has made this story appeal to audiences for so long?" EB: "I think it's that everyone has a secret dancer inside them that they dream will connect them to the physical world in the way they desire. It is in all of us waiting to be tapped."[1] A final note is that the hopeful, change-oriented political climate of the '60s is focused on more in the stage version than in the movie.

Several sources report that Mr. Josef Brown from Australia, who has been playing Johnny in the current stage show all over the world since 2004, has stated that the *Dirty Dancing* movie influenced him to pursue and to commit to a dance career. Per Sid Smith in the *Chicago Tribune*, September 28, 2008, Josef Brown said, "For kids like me, in a tough, all-boys school, the movie told of this guy who was a street kid and yet vulnerable too. It's OK to be masculine. But it's OK to dance as well."[3] There have been many other comments in the media as to how Mr. Swayze's portrayal of the character Johnny has encouraged and inspired men to dance.

On May 1 and 2, 2007, to celebrate the 20th anniversary of *Dirty Dancing*, there were showings of the Lionsgate new digital re-mastered 35mm print of *Dirty Dancing* with a twenty-minute clip about *Dirty Dancing* in about 330 theaters across the US, and 45 in Canada. Of course I attended, and was really struck by the varied age group of the audience and how everyone was really getting into the movie—myself included. From August 24–30, 2007, *Dirty Dancing* was shown at The Ziegfeld in New York (with a special Q & A with Kelly Bishop) to once again celebrate the twenty-year mark. In September and October 2007, a new show, *The Music of Dirty Dancing*, toured around the United Kingdom. On November 6, 2007, Mr. Swayze made a wonderful surprise appearance on *The Oprah Winfrey Show* to dance with Julia Boggio from the You Tube couple, Julia Boggio and James Derbyshire (from the United Kingdom). This couple's wedding video—which shows them doing the *Dirty Dancing* finale dance—had at that point been seen by more than two million You Tube viewers. At the end of 2007, *Dirty Dancing—The Video Game* was released by Codemasters.

Regarding other recent and/or ongoing *Dirty Dancing* activity, people from all over the world visit the locations where *Dirty Dancing* was filmed— Mountain Lake Hotel (Virginia) and Lake Lure Inn (North Carolina)—on a regular basis. (See separate sections on each location.) Mountain Lake Hotel has had *Dirty Dancing* weekends for years. In August 2007, Mountain Lake Hotel was the host of a United Kingdom television show—*Dirty Dancing: The Time of Your Life Reality Series-Season 1* in which ten one-hour episodes were filmed in thirty days. In June 2008, the filming of the second season of the show occurred. Ms. Miranda Garrison, the assistant choreographer and Vivian in the movie, was one of the judges for the shows. One of the most popular activities for guests at Mountain Lake throughout the years has been to have their picture taken with a life-size cutout picture of Patrick Swayze per Mr. H. M. "Buzz" Scanland, Jr., General Manager at Mountain Lake Hotel. In October 2007, *Seriously Dirty Dancing* (parts filmed at both Mountain Lake Hotel and Lake Lure Inn) a British documentary narrated by Dawn Porter (who reportedly saw the movie around 200 times) was aired.

In November 2008, *Dirty Dancing*: *The Ultimate Girls' Night in Collector's Pack* (DVD of movie, commentary, outtakes, and a night dress, washbag, eye mask, etc.) was released by Lionsgate. Also, in December 2008, the Lionsgate DVD, *Dirty Dancing: Official Dance Workout* became available. In March 2009, BBC aired *Let's Dance for Comic Relief* created by Whizz Kid Entertainment (United Kingdom). The show had contestants re-enact famous dances, which included a performance by Paddy McGuiness and Keith Lemon to "(I've Had) The Time of My Life" from *Dirty Dancing.* Money received from callers who voted for their favorite routines was given to Comic Relief. On August 19, 2009, multiple sources reported that per *Production Weekly*, Lionsgate is doing a remake of the movie. Only time will tell if this is indeed true. I think that you will find it interesting to read what the fans in this book say about a *Dirty Dancing* sequel—which may give some insight as to how popular a remake would be.

Thus, *Dirty Dancing* continues to go on and on. I can't resist commenting that this independent movie was made on a shoestring budget with virtually no violence (Johnny does briefly fight Robby in one scene), no special effects, no weirdness, and yet it has remained popular for over twenty years.

What makes *Dirty Dancing* such a phenomenon? For me, I know that all I have to do to get a quick shot of "feel-good" is throw the DVD in, sit back, and be captured by the bliss *of Dirty Dancing*. Whether I have been in a great mood and wanted a "fix," or whether I have been in a funk (like when my mother was laying in ICU, possibly going to die, about five years ago), I just had to pop in *Dirty Dancing* and could escape into a great place where there was love, integrity, and a happy ending. (I am not saying that seeing *Dirty Dancing* took away all of my stress regarding my mother's illness, but it did serve as an anchor to hope for me.) Furthermore, watching *Dirty Dancing* is kind of like meeting up with an old friend. Mr. Swayze spoke to *The Boston Globe's* Mark Shanahan in September 2005 about his and his wife's prized dance movie, *One Last Dance* (which they had just been to Slovakia to promote), and what he said can be applied to *Dirty Dancing* as well: "Everywhere we take this film, people want something to make them feel good. Hope is a big thing." He was also asked why audiences respond so strongly to dance. He said, "The world loves dance. It's our first form of worship. It's primal. Moving to rhythm is a powerful thing that's innate in all of us."[4] Mr. Swayze has made statements throughout the years that a big component of dancing with a partner is having a soul connection through the eyes. In his portrayal of Johnny and Ms. Grey's portrayal of Baby, the connection definitely happens, which is highlighted in one of the movie's songs, "Hungry Eyes" (written by Franke Previte and John De Nicola, and performed by Eric Carmen). By the way, the soundtrack to the movie has sold more than 42 million copies.

To think that Mr. Swayze almost didn't do *Dirty Dancing*! During the *ABC Barbara Walters Special Interview* in 1988, Mr. Swayze stated that he had been advised not to do the movie. However, he took the role because, "I felt something for Johnny, the guy from the streets . . . that is fighting to like himself, to believe in himself." It seems that Mr. Swayze put his own constant quest for personal/spiritual growth into the character of Johnny. He shared with Barbara Walters that he had backed off accepting "teenage idol" movie roles after *Skatetown USA* so that he could become a more accomplished actor. He said, "I was willing to bank on that with enough study and growth, and enough connection with myself and the truth in me, that I could become an actor to be reckoned with." Barbara Walters asked why do so many women watch the movie so many times. In response, he spoke about how the relationship between the two main characters was based on what is inside: "Everybody dreams that somebody would see into their lonely world . . . that would see past the exterior and see what they're really like . . . somebody sees through that and cares about them as a person . . . a relationship not because of how somebody swings their rear but because of what's inside . . ."[5]

Mr. Swayze has indicated throughout the years that key *to Dirty Dancing* is how Johnny and Baby connect with their hearts and souls, which is reflected in the movie's smash hit, "She's Like The Wind" (written by Mr. Swayze and Mr. Widelitz, and performed by Mr. Swayze, featuring Wendy Fraser). The song was #3 on *Billboard* Hot 100 and #1 on Adult Contemporary. In 1989, "She's Like The Wind" won at the BMI Film & TV Awards for "most performed song from a film." In April 2009, BMI (Broadcast Music, Inc.) reported that "She's Like The Wind" had officially charted its four millionth public performance. It is widely thought that Mr. Swayze was inspired by his wife in the writing of this hit song.

Per a June 5, 2006 *Whatsonstage.com* interview conducted by Terri Paddock in London, England—"Photos: Swayze & Sweeney Ready to Play in Dolls"—Mr. Swayze talked about the continuing popularity of the movie *Dirty Dancing.* "He (Mr. Swayze) attributes the success of 'the movie that wouldn't die' to the passion, and lack of ego, behind the original project . . . Mr. Swayze's words: 'When something works, it's really about heart.'"[6] Key *Dirty Dancing* people have indicated that Mr. Emile Ardolino's role as director was an important reason why *Dirty Dancing* worked so well—including his storytelling ability—especially by using dancing and humanness to make a film that touches the heart. Mr. Swayze has indicated in multiple media sources that Jennifer's Grey portrayal of Baby was totally amazing and really paramount to the movie.

Many of the principal people involved in creating/acting in *Dirty Dancing* have made statements to various media sources that they really enjoyed and appreciated the collaborative experience of making this movie. In a

September 2, 2008 interview by *FemaleFirst.co.uk*, "Miranda Garrison talks Dirty Dancing," Ms. Garrison was asked if she had fond memories of making *Dirty Dancing*. She replied, "My memories of making this film are fantastic. I honestly 'had the time of my life!' . . . We original 'Dirty Dance People' contributed so much of our personal life stories to this film. This 'collective' storytelling has become an enormous validation of our youth and artistic philosophy."[7] Of course, "(I've Had) The Time of My Life" (written by Frank Previte, Donald Markowitz, and John DeNicola and performed by Bill Medley and Jennifer Warnes) won an Oscar, a Grammy, and a Golden Globe in 1988.

Referencing the above-mentioned interview of Miranda Garrison, while responding to the question—did she know that the lift scene she choreographed would become such an iconic scene, Ms. Garrison's words give us additional insight into the collaborative nature of the filmmakers and why the movie is so successful. Ms. Garrison answered, "To set the record straight, Kenny Ortega, myself and likely Patrick Swayze presented many 'lifts' to the director Emile Ardolino and writer Elinor Bergstein. Emile and Elinor wanted a through-line metaphor for the ultimate triumph of both Baby and Johnny. Once this lift was found we all knew its narrative power. I am not surprised as much as pleased when 'story' as the root of dance is proved so effective."[7] A reviewer (unable to find the name of the reviewer) wrote that the collaboration of the extremely talented artists on the movie: "shows you the possibilities of music, dance, love and the movies are endless, and it leaves you in a dream state, contemplating the beauty not only of the film's artistry, but of the human talent and drive that enabled it."

In closing, I think that what Mr. Swayze told the *Telegraph.co.uk* in 2006 ("Patrick Swayze on 'Dirty Dancing'") about why *Dirty Dancing* has been so successful is really the bottom line: "It has been so successful because basically it's about love, and how the power of love can redeem us all."[8]

Two

THE "REAL" CATSKILLS PEOPLE
JACKIE HORNER
STEVE SCHWARTZ

INTRODUCTION

The story of *Dirty Dancing* takes place in the Catskills in 1963. The Catskills is a resort area less than two hours from New York City. The resort area has been affectionately nicknamed the "Borscht Belt" as in its heyday, there were more than 500 resorts open where many Jewish families vacationed and many Jewish entertainers performed—including Ms. Jennifer Grey's grandfather, Mr. Mickey Katz. The vacationing region turned into a cultural entity that became a very special and unique way of life. Also, many prominent people visited and performed at the resorts.

Initially, the Catskills resort area began as farms taking in guests and gradually developed into various vacation settings until it reached the above-mentioned 500 resorts (in an area of about 250 square miles) where reportedly for most of the 1990s, between a half million and one million Jewish people spent some summer vacation time there. Grossinger's and The Concord were two of the most prominent resorts in the Catskills. At the present time, there are only about twelve resorts still open.

Please enjoy the following two interviews in which Ms. Jackie Horner and Mr. Steve Schwartz share their experiences in the Catskills—particularly about their time at Grossinger's. You may be surprised to learn the impact of their experiences on the creation of *Dirty Dancing*. Let us remember also that Ms. Eleanor Bergstein spent time vacationing in the Catskills with her family as a teenager.

JACKIE HORNER

June 30, 2009, July 13, 2009 (written/letter interviews).
July 19, 2009 (telephone).

June 30, 2009—Letter from Ms. Jackie Horner.

Dear Sue,

Thank you for your call. I happen to live directly across the street from the famous Grossinger's Hotel where all the DD took place. Unfortunately, "they" wanted to film it there. However, the hotel was sold in 1986. I spent the summer of 1985 telling Eleanor Bergstein my story—going through photos of that era, clothing, and hair styles. The '60s was quite an era. I worked as the dance pro at Grossinger's from 1954 to 1986—then all the other hotels that were open. Now most are sold or closed.

I have my own studio in Liberty—lots of Ballroom, Salsa, Cha-cha, etc.

July 2009—Written interview.
Liberty, New York

I will try to answer your questions in order as written—plus.

Please tell me about the incidents of you carrying the watermelon.

Well, in the movie we had "Baby" (Jennifer Grey) carry the watermelon . . . however, it was me—the staff of waiters, waitresses, bellhops, maids etc. would have their parties to unwind. But the dance staff was considered upper crust—above them. We ate with the guests, used the outdoor pool where my upstairs dance studio was in the summer, sat in their cabanas. We taught and danced with them all day. Other staff couldn't even walk through the lobbies or bar areas—let alone the outdoor pool. So for us to crash their "fun time," we took offerings. So I would go to the kitchen and get a big watermelon and we would cut it up, "plug it," and pour vodka in the opening. Finally, after two or three times stealing it [watermelon] the chef put it out on a kitchen ledge for me with a note—"Have fun! It's our secret!"

I'm sure other hotels had their staff fun times and stories likewise—but I can only tell it like it happened with our staff of dancers . . . [And there was] so much more that wasn't even in the movie—story after story can be told.

Why do you think *Dirty Dancing* has remained so popular?

I think it has remained popular or even more so than when it opened because it's so bittersweet, and honest and true.

Then Ms. Horner proceeded to write me about other anecdotes and other information.

I just did a lecture on it and "outtakes of my own." Shelly Winters, bless her heart, was a dear friend and a Grossinger guest so often. One day she said, "Jackie, you are going to get hurt practicing your 'lifts' on these hard wood stages. Why don't you come down to the lake with me on Sunday and practice your dance lifts in the lake?" So I wrote that down, and it's a scene in the film.

Likewise, Eddie Fisher had a manager named Milton Blackstone, and one night in our Grossinger lounge, he spoke to me about my pupils—told me they were dancing too close. I said, "Milton they're doing a 'tango,' it's a close dance." "No," he said, "They're Dancing Dirty." Ahem, I wrote it down. This was all told to Eleanor and was put in the film and then some.

The strangest thing—just as I started this letter, out of the blue, my partner Steve Schwartz called. I just now hung up. He's the "Johnny" (Patrick Swayze). Weird—hadn't heard from him in months. He was blamed for everything and will be up to see us in early August. We've been on the phone for thirty minutes. He went by the name "Steve Sands"—still adorable at 72. You might want to interview him. He's in N.Y. City but travels back and forth to Florida.

Eleanor had hopes of filming it at Grossinger's but the hotel was sold in 1986 . . . But she said that I "breathed energy and life into the film and it came alive." Lots of ups and downs in the filming—wasn't easy! But now she has the musical all over the world—Australia, London, Germany, Spain, Toronto, Chicago, California casts.

Well, 1963 was the last summer Grossinger's had their staff show. It wasn't exactly a talent show. We had someone do an entire script and scenes—very little singing, acting . . . and I choreographed the dances for the hotel staff that cared to be in the show. We did it for the Labor Day weekend guests.

Funny, I was teaching the little couple that was stealing, and my partner was blamed for all that too. (*Jackie told me that she saw them stealing money and reported them, and of course she didn't get paid for sixteen lessons that she had taught them.*)

And I have a photo with Van Johnson who was here on a 1963 summer weekend. What a dear person, and of course loved to dance. All the "greats" in every field and walk of life graced the portals of Grossinger's.

Lou (*Lou Goldstein is Jackie's husband and is a legendary figure in his own right*) and I have done a documentary on Grossinger's . . . It's almost finished. The crew filmed all over.

Last Sunday I did the DD lecture at a museum up here—lovely turn out, and they showed the film.

And now it's the Bi-Centennial for the Catskills area. They showed the movie in our outdoor Park Pavilion last Saturday and I introduced it.

Last week, I spoke to the cast (actors, dancers) and the tech crew here at our fabulous Forestburgh Playhouse—summer stock at its best. They opened with the 1952 *Wish You Were Here*—the first Catskill musical done on Broadway years back. A super cast—all wanted to know about "those" years. It was fun to tell them stories about the "Activities Directors." It was my husband, Lou's job at the "G." In fact, in the film I have a "hair style wig show." I did that for him some afternoons when it was popular and still have those hairpieces. So theater is still strong here too. Did *All Shook Up*—Great! Last night I saw *Les Miserables*, and we do *Showboat* next, then *Rent* and *Hairspray* . . . Super season. Lots still to do here.

By the way, TNT did a filming for a few days up here while I was working at the Raleigh Hotel, and my partner and I re-created many scenes from the film and sequences, like walking on the log, watermelon bit up the steps, dance class (Merengue) at the pool, dancing Mambo in the night club. They inserted all the scenes in between the film DD where commercials would normally be. Was first shown December 19, 1999. And my interview as well.

So my dear Sue, I could go on and on. It was quite a time and still a good life continues. It was a special time, and so many still remember those perfect, sunny, happy days.

Ms. Horner sent me a copy of an article: "Film thrills Horner" from the *Times Herald-Record*, August 18, 1987, in which she was interviewed about *Dirty Dancing*. Here is one of the many interesting things that she told the reporter: "Several lines Penny says are mine." Also, she spoke to the reporter about what 1963 was like. "You could say 1963 was the last beautiful, innocent time." She also commented, "There was some sex among the hotel workers, but nothing like the movie showed. Honey, we were too tired to fool around . . . But we did do 'some dirty dancing' of our own after hours."[9]

ADDITIONAL BIOGRAPHICAL INFORMATION ON JACKIE HORNER

Here is an excerpt from: "Biographical Sketch—Jackie Horner."[10]

"Jackie Horner was born in a small town in southern Ohio to parents who were both active in musical endeavors. While she was engaged in modeling at the age of four, she, and her parents became increasingly aware of her love for music accentuated by the beat of her dancing feet. They knew that her future would be transcended beyond the sphere of the posing little Miss Horner.

Hence, the dance was soon to capture Jackie's total interest. She was to study beyond the norm under such celebrated dance masters as Grace Bedell, Deborah London Hoffman, Henry Le Tang, Jose Limon, and Jack Stanley in New York; and Carol Linn of the Peabody Conservatory of Music in Baltimore."

The sketch also states that Ms. Horner was a Rockette and a member of the June Taylor dance company. "Ms. Horner has danced throughout the United States, Canada, Mexico and South America in night clubs, theaters, and television's top variety shows . . . At present, she teaches dance here in the Catskills, colleges, regional theaters, and choreographs musical theater productions as well as appearing in some . . . The Catskills are her magical mountains, where her happiest moments have been spent teaching the stars of Hollywood, television and all the guests who come on vacations these many years."

STEVE SCHWARTZ (Steve Sands—professional dancer name)

Lives in New York, NY.

August 1, 2009 (telephone interview).
August 17, 2009 (e-mail follow-up question).

Ms. Jackie Horner had told me that the character, Johnny in the movie, *Dirty Dancing* was based on you. Is that true?

Well, you know, much of the film was things that were involved with Jackie . . .

A lot of the what we call shtick, a lot of the stuff—that he did was my stuff—which I didn't recognize . . . Everybody's telling me that there's a movie about a dance teacher in the Catskills, that I should go see it. So I went to see it. And I sat down and I watched the movie. You know, it's like if Julio went to see a movie about Julio. He says yeah, that's the way it was, that's the way it was. Absolutely nothing registered with me.

At the end of the film, I get up to leave and my wife said, "Let's look at the call. I don't recognize the hotel." 'Cuz she and I met in the Catskills. So I'm sitting there and all of a sudden I see a full screen with special thanks to Jackie Horner. And I go my God, I know what this is—this is about Jackie and I. The next morning I call Liberty . . . I get Lou Goldstein's and Jackie's telephone number. Lou gets on the phone . . . "Lou, this is Steve Schwartz, Steve Sands (I used the name Sands when I was a dancer). He said to me: "Oh, how'd you like the movie Steve?" OK . . .

Now, conversely, I was up in the Catskills with Jackie for a few dance weekends and she introduced me as the guy that Johnny was based on. A great part of that film—the essence of that film—was the information that Jackie gave to Eleanor Bergstein.

Uh-huh.

However, there was another dancer (another very well known dancer probably better known than I was) by the name of Michael Terrace. Michael and I are very close friends and partners in a film venture that we're working on. We go back many, many years. And Eleanor Bergstein says that she developed the character of Johnny from Michael Terrace. And Michael Terrace gave her different ideas about the film as well. So if you ask me, I think it is a juxtaposition of Michael and I . . . They had a thing on TV about *Dirty Dancing*. Eleanor Bergstein was on, the producers were on, and Michael was on, and she said it on television: "I based the character, Johnny on Michael Terrace." Subsequently, I've been with Eleanor Bergstein . . . We talked about it . . . She said, "Yeah, you know I don't know if it was you but you know, it was somewhere in the stuff, the stories that Jackie told me." So I think Johnny is a juxtaposition of Michael and I—which is probably news to you.

Yeah—definitely.

I can put you in touch with Michael as well . . . And Michael is convinced that he is, you know, he's the guy . . .

Wow, that's amazing. I wonder why more people don't know about it.

Well, people really don't know about anything. They really don't know about Michael. They really don't know about me or Jackie . . . I am giving you what I believe is the real story relevant to who the film was based on—the male character . . . Even the dance steps in there that are my steps . . .

Oh, my gosh!

Jackie had a lot of influence. The stuff that came from Jackie which she got a full screen for—was about she and I. Michael never had a screen and didn't have a full credit on it. So Jackie really was the major influence relevant to the information that went on.

OK. Wow. So looking at your background what was it like being a dancer, being a male in those times?

Well, you know everybody you're talking to—Jackie and Lou, and even Mike—they were at least ten years older than I am. I got my first job as a dance instructor at a place called Laurel Pines in Lakewood. I got there and I had just turned sixteen. I told them I was nineteen or twenty and I took a leave from school. I ran away from home. I never went to high school or anything like that. I was a terrific dancer. So when I finished the season—you know the name, Tisch? This was their first hotel and first venture—Bob and Larry Tisch . . . They became world renown, very philanthropic and everything. I was going to their summer resort—a place called The Grand at Highmount, Highmount, New York, which is near Fleischman in the Catskills. And I did a show at Roseland . . . This is the spring of 1954 . . . I was seventeen . . .

So we did the show, and I came off stage and a dance couple by the name of Tony and Lucille (Colon) come over to me. They were really famous . . . They are really very high class, and they said to me, "How would you like to come to work for me at Grossingers?" It was like they said to me *how would you like to go to work at The Palace?* Top of the top—of the top. I went to work at Grossinger's in the spring of 1954, at the age of seventeen—telling them that I was twenty.

When I got to Grossinger's, they put me together with Jackie as my partner. What was it like? First of all, I thought I died and went to heaven. Here I am a kid from Brooklyn. My father had passed away when I was twelve years old . . . I was lying my way through my life as far as my age and what my background was, and here I wind up in the number one luxurious place in the Jewish American world . . . If I may say so, I was probably the better dancer there . . . I was really a very good dancer . . . By the way, Mike Terrace is also a brilliant dancer. The activity was getting people to give lessons to, rehearsing for Friday night's champagne hour, and winding up with girls at night. That was the major activity.

Are you still teaching dancing?

No, the last forty odd years, I own a construction company.

Do you still dance?

Very, very rarely. Once in awhile I'll go with Mike Terrace . . . It's rare. I would say if I go half a dozen times a year, at a max ten times a year. I made a video with Barry Manilow about ten years ago called "Hey Mambo" . . . that I was the lead dancer on . . .

So how old were you when you first started dancing?

When my father was alive, we used to spend the entire summer in the Catskills. My father was a dental oral surgeon. And we were pretty well off . . . My father and mother were wonderful dancers—as well as my sister. My sister was four years older than me. So I used to watch them dance, and I danced. I was put on stage the first time when I was four or five years old . . . I sang. I danced. I did all that stuff. As I got older, I used to go with my friends, to different dances with the girl. I was always the best dancer—that was before the time of the Mambo . . . I did the Lindy Hop . . . The girls would say, "Can you show me how to do the Lindy Hop?"

So my identity started to develop as a dancer. When my father passed away when I was twelve, I lost it. I was very, very close to my father. I didn't go to school . . . No one wanted to hang out with me. Parents didn't want their children to play with me 'cuz I was a bad influence, etc. etc. And a great insecurity grew in me . . . I had little going for me. And dancing seemed to be the only thing that I was admired for . . . I left home when I was sixteen. All of a sudden, I was somebody special. I was a dancer—better than anybody else. And being exposed to the level of people because of the hotels I was at—Laurel Pines, Concord, Grossinger's, hotels in Miami Beach, Americana—all those big hotels. I was with the wealthiest, most cultured people in the world. The exposure to them, plus some of the friendships I made over the years afforded me a different type of education and sophistication, which I never could have obtained had I not been a dancer. My dancing was a vehicle to my growth and education. I was demeaned by my own thoughts of myself, plus people would say to me, "What's a nice Jewish boy like you being a dance instructor? . . . You should be in school—you should be a doctor, a lawyer, a dentist." So that became my raison d'etre: what I wanted to do, what I wanted to become, as opposed to being a dancer.

By the way, I write poetry. I write lyrics. I do many, many things which really I should have stayed in show business all these years because that's what I was meant to do. I have had success in my construction career. I have lived a very nice life. So that's what dancing did for me. Dancing was my college. People say where did you go to school, and I say Grossinger's . . . I said I went to graduate school at the Fountain Bleu, Eden Rock . . . I left dancing at the end of the fifties. You know—started developing my skills in my construction business and moved on.

So you were not like Johnny in the movie. You did not teach at Arthur Murray's?

Arthur Murray was the dancing school for almost everybody in the cities and the towns . . .

So what dances were popular during that time period?

During the period of *Dirty Dancing?*

Yes.

Well the big dance was the Mambo, and the Cha-cha, and the Merengue . . . Mambo number one. The Cha–cha came along—I would say about 1953–54. Mambo was first—originally, it was the Rhumba. The Mambo started around 1948—places like the China Door, and then of course the place where the Mambo really was fantastic was the Palladium. I was going to the Palladium when I was thirteen years old in Roseland. I was a precocious kid . . . The Merengue came out of Santa Domingo around the same time. That's a cultural dance of [the] Dominican Republic. You know, it's been there a hundred years . . . The Mambo came out of Cuba . . . Now what we are talking about is not what happened—or the *Dirty Dancing* era if you will . . . The dancers from our time were all very creative. Everybody had a different style . . . Everybody did different steps. It was a great era. The Mambo jamborees and all the hot stuff that was going on between New York and Miami was fantastic and it created tremendous excitement . . .

So as far as the *Dirty Dancing* is concerned, there were all kinds of dynamics that went on in the dance studio. You work for an hour or a half-hour with a woman and her husband, or a woman alone, or a man alone . . . And you're dancing close to each other and all kinds of possibilities start to come up—which you can imagine . . . which was an ongoing thing. It was ridiculous. The husbands would go away during the week, and they'd come up for the weekend. The wife would be running around—carrying on during the week. That was one of the major activities.

Oh, so that part of the movie is true?

Oh, without a doubt.

Bungalow Bunnies?

Oh definitely. The two major hotels up there were Grossinger's and the Concord. Very tight security. So the "Bungalow Bunnies" were not allowed to come on the grounds . . .

"Bungalow Bunnies" were not guests at the hotels. They lived for the summer in bungalow colonies which were a much lower economic situation than the hotels. The husbands, working men, came up on weekends. They tried to sneak into the hotels for the entertainment, dancing, and mid-week sex. There were little or no bunnies at Grossinger's or the Concord since the security was very tight. At the smaller hotels, they were a factor. They made the staff (waiters and busboys) very happy. A very small number of bunnies may have gotten into the bigger hotels, but very few.

I'm talking about the guests at the hotel. The guests at the hotel conducted themselves as much or more so than the "Bungalow Bunnies" . . . And who else but with the dance instructors because the waiter staff and bellboy staff at these hotels were not permitted to mingle with the guests . . . At the small hotels, it was a free-for-all . . . Here, all you had were people on the athletic staff, or the dancers or the musicians, office people for the ladies to get involved with, or the ladies' daughters or sons. That was a major activity. A lot of that went on. And you can imagine, a seventeen–eighteen year old kid—who wasn't too bad looking.

WOW . . .

. . . the kind of education I got . . . The women offering money and all that. That's all very true. It all happened. Big time. Big time.

So because of the Security at Grossinger's and the Concord, there weren't the Bungalow Bunnies, but it was the wives and the daughters.

Let me tell you a few stories about the Baby situation . . . Baby checked in every Friday and checked out the following Sunday, and new Babies checked in. And it wasn't just Baby. It was Baby's mother who took a lesson and we got involved with, and it was Baby's aunt, and it was Baby's grandmother . . . And this went on every week. Sometimes they stayed two weeks, sometimes they stayed a month. But there was always a fresh crop. I'm telling you this is what it was like.

The guys took much more advantage of it than the female guests . . . The girls weren't anywhere as near promiscuous as the working guys were.

And the scene with the dance kids—the last dance at the end of the year—that's a made-up thing . . . I'm sure Jackie told you that . . .

We didn't get into that . . .
She (Jackie) told me about the watermelon though—how it was laced with Vodka.

Yeah . . . Where we, the dancers went after work, most of the time was a restaurant in Liberty, New York called Corey's. Corey's had the best Chinese food you ever tasted in your life, and they had the best band in the world. It's owned by Betty and Marty Corey . . . We would go there and we would dance until the sun came up . . . Dancing and working and eating all day, having three meals a day at the hotel. We'd go and have Chinese food later and dance some more . . . All the dancers from all the different hotels . . . On Thursday night, they had a marvelous jamboree there.

You talked about the last dance. What about the lift scene—when Johnny lifts Baby up in the air? You know, they practiced in the lake.

It's interesting that you mention that—that's what Mike Terrace gave to Eleanor Bergstein. The broken window in the car—Mike Terrace. The lift in the water—Mike Terrace . . . I think he gave her four to five scenes.

In Jackie's stuff, I think there was something about Shelly Winters telling her, "Why are you practicing the lifts here, you can get hurt? Why don't you practice in the water?" Maybe they could have both had input into it.

I wasn't there. Mike didn't go down there with them. Mike didn't get any credit. Mike didn't get any mention. Jackie got a full screen credit . . . that's big time . . . There's a lot of Jackie in there . . . You know it's fifty-four years . . . memories . . . Again when you ask Eleanor Bergstein who the character of Johnny was, she'll say Mike Terrace. You ask Jackie Horner who the character of Johnny was, she'll say Steve Schwartz/Steve Sands . . . I only met Eleanor a few years ago. Mike and I are working on a movie script about the Palladium in the fifties—which we've been working on for the last two years . . . You know dancing has become very popular.

That's another question I had. I read all over the place—newspaper articles, magazines—after *Dirty Dancing* came out, a lot more people signed up for dancing lessons.

Yeah, sure. I am quite sure they did. Look at the biggest shows on television. *Dancing with the Stars* or *So You Think You Can Dance*. They are marvelous shows, absolutely marvelous. To me especially *So You Think You Can Dance*. I think you see the most wonderful dancing and most exciting dancing. *Dancing with the Stars* is also a terrific show which is exciting. It is more publicly doable . . . the public can do what they're doing on *Dancing with the Stars*—the public is inclined to take lessons and learn how to dance. That's bigger than ever. Bigger than our years because our years were limited to the resorts in the Catskills or Miami Beach or LA. Predominantly, it happened no place else for all those years. It was very, very big in those places. It was the major activity—watching it or taking lessons or you know—all that stuff . . .

What years would you say that occurred?

The fifties.

I have another question. Why do you think—from your perspective— *Dirty Dancing* is still so popular? It is on all of the time. People are into it.

You know what Shakespeare said: "The play's the thing." It was just a terrific story. Boy meets girl. Boy loses girl. Boy gets girl back . . .

It really is a formula movie and formulas work. The dancing was simple enough and easy enough for people to associate it with it and say gee, I can do that . . . There was summer romance.

Just think about it. Jennifer Grey . . . you know who her father is . . . She looked terrific in the movie. There was a little bit of sex, but it really wasn't heavy sex. It just had those little components—those feelings of being away in a hotel and not being around your normal surroundings . . . It just rang the bell in different directions. You had a villain—the guy who got the girl pregnant. You had a hero—Johnny. He was very attractive in that film. He was most dynamic in that movie—just wonderful. You know with the leather jacket and the collars turned up and the hair popping over—which we looked like.

Really?

To some extent. You'll see the pictures . . . Why so popular? It was believable. I think that was it more than anything else . . . The old couple stealing something.

I heard that was true. That's another thing, Jackie Horner said you would get blamed for things.

That's correct . . . I was a little kid. In fact, I had one woman—she accused me of trying to come on to her, and I mean—she was a season guest, came for years and years, and season guests were like god-fare . . . Most people came up for the weekend or a week.

There was a stealing thing also?

It wasn't stealing—it was more I was making advances to her. It was absolutely not true. And she went to Jenny Grossinger, you know the big boss, and tried to get me fired. Lucille stood up for me and I didn't get fired . . . I was a sixteen–seventeen year old kid in a highly sophisticated adult world.

There's a similar issue in the movie. He (Johnny) was becoming a plasterer or something in construction. Well, I wound up in construction. That part of it is true. The dancing afterward at night is very true . . . The girls and the Baby part is very true—where there were relationships with girls, and girls getting pregnant.

Mr. Schwartz then e-mailed me pictures of himself dancing at Grossinger's and other Catskills hotels, and other major dance hotels in Miami Beach and LA from about 1953–1957. We looked at the pictures (on our respective computers).

The next one is the Champagne hour . . . We had a champagne hour every Friday night. We were the show on Friday night. First, we would do some exhibitions. Then we'd have people come up and we'd have a contest—they'd dance different dances and have applause and whoever won got a bottle of champagne. All the hotels did that . . .

I thought this would give you the flavor of what it was like for Johnny—
what his life was like . . .

*Mr. Schwartz asked me to tell him about myself. In the course of the
discussion, I told Mr. Schwartz about my involvement in The Official
Patrick Swayze International Fan Club. Mr. Schwartz commented that
he knew that during the '40s and '50s, there were a lot of fan clubs for
movie stars.*

I didn't know that still existed.

**I don't think there is another club like this one . . . Patrick and Lisa
personally send pictures and information to the club . . . Many of the
fans are very good friends . . .**

He comes across as a very, very fine young man . . . He's such a lovely
young man, and I think this [pancreatic cancer] to happen to him is so,
so terrible . . .

*We talked some more about various subjects. At the end of the
interview, I thanked Mr. Schwartz, and he thanked me because he said
it brought back years that were very, very special to him.*

WRAP UP OF INTERVIEWS OF MS. HORNER AND MR. SCHWARTZ

Obviously, Ms. Eleanor Bergstein did indeed capture the special time that took place in the Catskills heyday and all of the information that was given to her by all parties involved. Finally, let us not forget that Ms. Eleanor Bergstein also spent summers there.

Per Veronica Lee in her article, "There's a secret dancer inside us all" (*Guardian News and Media, 2006*) regarding *Dirty Dancing*:

"For Bergstein, much of it is autobiographical. 'I was a teenager in 1963, we were New York Jewish, I was a doctor's daughter with one older sister and we took holidays in the Catskills . . . My father practiced in a poor area and charged only a dollar a consultation,' she says."

(Me: Now here comes something else to think about pertaining to the creation of the character of Johnny.) Eleanor Bergstein, "So we never had much money. Johnny who comes from the wrong side of the tracks and scratches a living as a dancing teacher represents the 'otherness I felt.'"[11]

Three

MOUNTAIN LAKE HOTEL

INTRODUCTION

How can one write a book on *Dirty Dancing* without visiting the film location at Mountain Lake Hotel in Pembroke, Virginia?

So off I headed to the famous site where the Houseman family pulled up in their car to the main lodge, Johnny entered the dining room and told the college boy where to put the pickle, Penny crouched down crying on the floor in the corner of the kitchen, Baby and Johnny practiced their lift in the lake, Johnny danced with Vivian in the gazebo, and on and on . . . If only I could have had this idea in the summertime or maybe even spring. No, not me—I ventured out in four below zero weather (January 12–14, 2009) trekking through the snow taking in the sights and atmosphere of Mountain Lake. Mr. H.M. "Buzz" Scanland Jr., General Manager (known as Buzz) at Mountain Lake Hotel was gracious enough to be a host to me for two days showing me the famous spots and archives regarding *Dirty Dancing*—including a script, pictures, videos, and documents, and most helpful of all telling me stories about all that went on during the filming of *Dirty Dancing*. I will be forever grateful to Mr. Scanland for his participation in this project.

It was just totally amazing being on the grounds of the property where much of *Dirty Dancing* was filmed. In a sense, it was very surreal and at the same time, it was like it was meant to be—that I had come home. It was also very bittersweet because I was still so totally blown away by Mr. Swayze's performance in *Dirty Dancing* (watched excerpts in the videos there on a big screen) and still so very sad about his illness. (I was glad that I was watching the *Dirty Dancing* clips by myself, so that I could cry as much as I wanted.) It all came back to me as to how much the movie has done for me and how much of a classic *Dirty Dancing* has become for me and countless others. First, the movie helped me get over the hurdle of the end of the relationship with my so-called soul mate, and then it became like an old friend in times of need or just a great, feel-good time. Coming to Mountain Lake was like taking one more step of living my dream of writing this book. I can't resist saying that one of the messages in *Dirty Dancing* is to go after what you want and stand up for what you believe in. There is a similar message in *One Last Dance* (the movie written, directed, starred in, and produced by Ms. Niemi and starred in and produced by Mr. Swayze) which is—it is never too late to make your dreams come true. The essence of these messages really hit home while I was at Mountain Lake.

MOUNTAIN LAKE HOTEL LOCATION INFORMATION

It was obvious from the start that filming in the Catskills was not going to be possible due to budgetary constraints as the filmmakers had to make the movie for under five million dollars. The producers had already found Lake Lure Inn in North Carolina. Then in June 1986, the *Dirty Dancing* producers saw Mountain Lake Hotel in Pembroke, Virginia in an advertisement in Piedmont Airlines in-flight magazine, and went there and decided to make it the film's Kellerman's Resort. The movie was filmed at Mountain Lake from September 5 to September 20, 1986. Most of the exterior scenes were shot there as well as some interior scenes, including the outside of the main lodge, the kitchen, the dining room, the gazebo, the beach, the Houseman cottage (Virginia Cottage), and the lift scene in the lake (shot in about 30 degree weather). Most of the cast stayed at Mountain Lake—at least some of the time. Mr. Swayze stayed in Room 232 and Ms. Grey in Room 513. (See list of guests and room assignments.)

Regarding the history of Mountain Lake, it started out as a resort in around 1857. The stone lodge was built in 1936. The beautiful Mountain

Lake 2,600 acreage (of which 2,455 acres are forests) is 4,000 feet above sea level in the Appalachian Mountains in Giles County, Virginia. Per the Mountain Lake Hotel website: "The Mountain Lake Conservancy is a non-profit organization founded in 1989 to help manage and protect the 2,600 acres of Mountain Lake Property and to provide environmental and cultural education to the public . . . Our mission is to further Mary Moody Northern's desire to forge bonds between people and nature in Mountain Lake's unique environment."[12] The natural lake on the property is amazing because of how high up on the mountain it is and also it is one of only two fresh water lakes in the state. The water level is cyclical—high and low depending on how much rain and snowfall occur. In April 2009, the lake was rising again, and by July 2009, it was up to 43' below full pond. With the snowfall from Winter 2010, the lake is said to be slowly rising again.

I had the absolute pleasure of interviewing Mr. H. M. "Buzz" Scanland Jr., General Manager, and Mr. Mike Porterfield, Executive Chef, regarding the filming of *Dirty Dancing* at Mountain Lake.

BUZZ SCANLAND

January 16 & 17, 2009.

In-person interviews at Mountain Lake Hotel, Pembroke, Virginia.

Introduction: E-mail to me from Buzz, December 4, 2008.

If you have not been here, you should come. Also, have you seen the stage play? I thought it was great. I saw it in Toronto. It is now playing in Chicago and will open next year in Boston. You would not believe how many people come here just because of *Dirty Dancing*. The weekend before Thanksgiving, we had a *Dirty Dancing* Weekend and one couple came from England and another couple from Toronto. We get guests for *Dirty Dancing* from all over the world.

The first part of the interview on January 16th was done while Buzz was driving me to my first visit to Mountain Lake.

What was your position with Mountain Lake when *Dirty Dancing* was filmed?

I had just come to Mountain Lake. I was doing marketing. My first few weeks on the job were when *Dirty Dancing* was filmed.

Who in the cast did you have contact with?

I had minimal contact with Jerry Orbach and Jack Weston—like "hi"— that was it.

I met Jennifer Grey once and hadn't even known who she was. Supposedly, Jennifer's father, Joel Grey, sent Jennifer flowers every day. I didn't have any contact with Buddy.

You know, Patrick wanted to be called Buddy.

When *Dirty Dancing* was being made, did you think it would be a big hit?

No. Nobody did.

While filming, were there guests in the hotel?

Yes, and we had to be careful regarding the noise.

Where did the movie people eat?

They ate where the guests did.

They would bus the extras over and give them lunch and $50.00 for all day.

The first choice for extras was for Jewish people from Blacksburg.

They would pay $100.00 a day for a vintage car to be in the movie.

There was a '57 Chevy owned by Jan Gilley that was used in the movie. Buddy drove this car.

I'm getting excited! (We were rapidly approaching Mountain Lake.)

Everybody that you talk to has heard of *Dirty Dancing*.

Of course.

Especially if you're a young female . . . and we get a lot of telephone calls. They will ask us, "Is this where *Dirty Dancing* was filmed?" and we say, "Yeah" . . . and they'll say, "This is where I want to come because I'm bringing my wife because she's into that movie so much."

Are you trying to tell me that the women like it more than the men?

Oh yeah . . .

It's like when I saw it in Toronto—the stage play. The tickets were sent to me . . . the seats were down front about five or six rows. My two grandsons liked it . . . This lady was there with her husband . . . She said, "Well, my husband didn't think it was such a great play."

It's a female movie . . . no doubt about it . . . but you get so many guys because their wives are into it, they are into it . . .

I interviewed one young man whose mom was really into it. She constantly played it in their house. He likes it, but I don't think he likes it as much as his mom. (I interviewed his mom also.)

You know something, Mallory Longworth . . . she would never have come here if it wouldn't have been for a teenage girl who was here with her parents, and she saw we were having a *Dirty Dancing* weekend. Then she saw an article (in *Newsweek*) about Mallory. She got on the phone . . . evidently there are two Mallory Longworths in the Detroit area and on the second phone call, she got a hold of Mallory . . . and that's the reason Mallory came down here. (See interview of Mallory Longworth.)

That is amazing!

That little girl is from Virginia. I couldn't tell you what her name is . . .

I would love to find out who she is—you know because she was probably fifteen to eighteen then, and now she is thirty-five to thirty-eight—a little bit older. I would love to know what her reaction is towards *Dirty Dancing*. So you might ask Mallory . . . Mallory came twice for the *Dirty Dancing* weekends. (**Note: Buzz came up with the idea to have *Dirty Dancing* weekends.**)

We are getting closer . . .

We are on the backside now . . .

Snow . . .

We had somebody come here and stay a week last fall . . . and I think they were from Italy . . . and they just came up here because of the movie . . . Well, it's nine degrees right now . . . When I came up this morning, it was eight below . . .

Well, it sure is pretty . . . it is beautiful . . . can't imagine—you know the summertime . . .

Oh, my goodness . . . oh, my goodness . . .

It's kind of funny, Miranda Garrison, when she came up here to do the movie, she stayed in one of these cottages . . . and that is where all of the dancers stayed when they came to make the television series (the UK show *Dirty Dancing: The Time of Your Life*). Miranda Garrison stayed in 315 . . .

When they did the television series, we used this house out here . . . The winners of the dance-off, they would come out here and have a special dinner with champagne and so forth . . .

Well, it's gone back to six degrees . . .

Wow, a regular heat wave . . . very pretty . . .

They came in here and showed the hotel . . .

Oh my gosh.

From this angle—like they were coming to the hotel . . . and before we widened the road . . . they really came in the opposite way . . . it used to be one way around the hotel . . . you went in on the back side and came out on the front side, but now we widened this road since the movie. Also, these ballers and chains—they put those in to start with, and we have maintained them.

Awesome.

Of course, they parked here—right in front of the hotel.

Yes. "I don't think I brought enough shoes."

That's the cottage right over there, and of course, we changed it around. It's got a stone wall in front of it and the porch used to come off the front of it, and that's the one the Housemans stayed in. It's called Virginia

Cottage. She (Baby) came out in front of it and came across the lawn . . . and came up to the hotel.

We went inside to the lobby . . . Oh, look at the poster!

I have one upstairs too . . . Somebody gave me that one . . . You can't find Patrick Swayze cut-outs anymore . . .

Buzz shows me this huge book that has *Dirty Dancing* information, and says:

And these are contracts to the movie, and these are some drawings for the sets, the beach . . .

What are those?

These are the rooms. This is the system. In other words, Jane Brucker . . . She was in Room 103 . . . Jerry Orbach was in 117, Jack Weston was in 119, Lonnie Price was in 201 . . . I've got the original where they signed in . . .

Oh my gosh.

Kenny Ortega, Miranda Garrison, Jennifer Gilbert . . . every name is twice because the way you do it, the company pays for the room and the incidentals are paid for by the person . . .

Here's some more information on where they were staying . . . Here's your script . . .

Oh, my goodness, I can't believe it.

Here are some pictures that we have . . . like Jennifer Grey talking to someone . . .

Oh, my goodness. Who took the pictures?

We probably took them ourselves . . . See we had a bridge almost similar to the one in North Carolina, and the funny part is we tore it out in between the time they made the movie and when the movie came out.

There they are down by the beach . . .

Everybody has sweaters on.

JANUARY 17, 2009

Why do you think the movie is so popular?

It's a feel-good movie. You know, it comes out good in the end. I think it's going to be a classic. Maybe in another ten to fifteen years there will be a re-make.

Buzz told me that he took the contestants from the UK dance reality show to the river (twenty minute drive) in a bus for the lifts and got to know them well—got close to them. He said that was the same location that Dawn Porter used for her lifts. (Dawn Porter did the UK Documentary: Seriously Dirty Dancing in 2007).

Then when they came in the second time (2008), I was really close to the people who were in charge . . . the producers, the lady that was overseeing everything . . . you know—the day to day dealing with them.

Of course, Miranda (who was a judge) I talked to, Sean (Cheesman, who was a judge) I talked to the third judge, Kelly Brook—she is the girlfriend of Billy Zane—who played in *Titantic*. She played in *Smallville*. She's English. But I never really had any long conversations with her.

How long did they stay?

About a month . . . each time.

Miranda—she was a super nice person when she was here. She talked to the other guests. As a matter of fact, she enjoyed her time here. She was into the movie since she was part of it and you do know the story behind it, you saw part of it in Dawn's show. It was my understanding, the lady (Lynn Lipton) who was going to play the mother got sick and she wanted to see her personal doctor in New York . . . so she took off and flew back to New York. So Kelly Bishop, Vivian, the "Bungalow Bunny"—she dropped out of that part and took the mother's part (Marjorie Houseman). I guess maybe somebody told her she would be better off if she took the mother's part—it was a better part than playing the "Bungalow Bunny" . . . Miranda was just here as a choreographer and helping with the dancing. She of course had acting experience. Miranda stepped into that role of Vivian . . . which is almost like an accident. I thought the best part in the movie was Vivian. I guess because of age and everything . . . it kind of appealed to me . . . and I just thought that Miranda did a fantastic job. **(NOTE: There is a scene in the beginning of the movie that Lynn Lipton is in briefly, which was shot the first day. She is riding in the car with the rest of the Housemans as they approach Kellerman's, and you just see the top of her head.)**

They were on such a small budget. I think they had five million dollars (so had to fill the roles quickly). They were on a tight schedule. There was no doubt about it.

I just came up here to do marketing. Like I said, I wasn't really involved in making the movie. If you did something like that again, you're probably better off to almost shut everybody out of the hotel.

Definitely.

We've had a lot of things come our way because of *Dirty Dancing* . . . We did a commercial for Wrangler Jeans on the lake. We did outdoor furniture by the lake—a lot of things. High Rollers, Wheel of Fortune, Jeopardy, Concentration . . . all those things came about to give us free publicity . . . Piedmont Airlines and *PACE* magazine . . . they gave us on a contest, the back cover of the magazine. I mean Piedmont Airlines was pretty big in those days, before US Air bought them out . . .

We got a lot of publicity here, there, and yonder.

And right now, again it has come back because of the stage play in Toronto. We were on the radio up there.

Oh really.

. . . just last year . . . in fact, the winners of the contest came here in November [2008] to the *Dirty Dancing* weekend. They flew down.

What did they win?

They won an airline trip from Toronto to Roanoke. They were doing it to promote the stage play . . .

So anyway, and right now since it is playing in Chicago, we are probably going to try to work out something with the Chicago radio station, and maybe in turn work out something with the radio station in Roanoke to do a contest where the ones in Roanoke win a trip to Chicago to see the stage play, and the people in Chicago win a *Dirty Dancing* weekend to come to Mountain Lake.

That would be great.

I just think it is a deal that really promotes us. We got quite a few people from Canada this year and then England, you know, coming for *Dirty Dancing* weekends or coming any other time. And right now with the lake being down, our biggest hook is *Dirty Dancing*.

When did the lake go down?

I'm saying this . . . I may not be exactly right. I think it went down the first time in 2003 or it may have been 2001 . . . It went down to probably 2/3 its size . . . It came back and then started down again over a period of time until it went completely dry about the end of August, first of September . . . it went completely dry. And now of course, it is coming back. So I am hoping that it will fill back up because it just makes it so much nicer here when the lake is full. It is really a beautiful lake and it is pristine . . . it's clear water . . . many, many moons ago, they used to pump the water right straight out of the lake for drinking water . . . They probably put a little chlorine in it . . . I wouldn't drink it now because you know we have a lot of animals around the edges . . .

What kind of animals are around here today?

We have black bear, rabbits, raccoons, umpteen million deer . . .

I saw some tracks today.

You've got fox, coyotes, rabbits, skunks, possums, weasels . . . There's a little bit of everything in this area . . . squirrels, chipmunks—they call them boomers and the boomers look like about the size of chipmunks but have thin, fuzzy tails, and they are aggressive—trying to get food off the table . . . We have a couple of cats that keep the boomers out . . . The boomers are really the only bad news that we really have . . . There's all kinds of snakes . . . but as long as I have been here, I have not seen a snake on a trail or anywhere.

I have a question . . . just to clarify things . . . Was the gazebo used when Johnny was dancing at night with Vivian? Did they use it also for the line dance when Baby stepped on the guy's foot?

Yes, that was in the gazebo—that was when they first came here. The other scene that I can remember right now is the scene when her father was sitting there and she goes up to him.

But there was a scene when Baby came to get Johnny to let him know that Penny was upset in the kitchen?

That was at the gazebo.

So that's three right there.

And if you remember, they crossed the chains on the ballers—what you saw this morning . . . stepped over the chains . . . all three of them— Johnny, his cousin, Baby . . . coming up to get Penny. *(Buzz had shown me this morning the wooden fence posts with a chain strung through them that were put in by the movie people.)*

This is just totally amazing!

They bought furniture that you see in the movie that's out on the lawn

. . . they were just for the scenes . . . Of course, they put up those little lanterns—like I showed you right there—all over the place. You see those throughout the movie . . .

Another thing I thought was neat, is if you looked at the awnings on the hotel, they were peach and white, and they go all the way across the porch and the entrance way . . . but when you're watching the movie, you know they can be here and walk inside and then they're in Lake Lure. I mean things just go back and forth. And when they're in Lake Lure, one time, I think when they were playing cards, Moe, who I think was his name, Vivian's—the Bungalow Bunny's husband—anyway you can look out the window that's down there, and you'll see the peach and white awnings. In other words, they carried the theme through . . . Also, they had hairdressers. If I am not mistaken, they hired some of the hairdressers out of Blacksburg, and then when they went to North Carolina, they took them with them.

You said before I think that the dance scenes were done at Lake Lure.

Yes.

I think that I am speechless.

MIKE PORTERFIELD

AGE 51. VIRGINIA.

March 2009 (telephone interview) & May 2009 (e-mail follow-up).

What was your position with Mountain Lake Hotel when *Dirty Dancing* was filmed there?

Well, at that time, I was the lead line cook . . . I ran the dinner line. We worked from 7am until closing at night . . . with breaks.

How old were you?

I was about age twenty-eight or twenty-nine.

How long had you worked there at that point?

That was my third season there.

You and your family have a connection with Mountain Lake that goes way back. Could you share something about that?

My family owned it in the late 1880s.

Your family owned it?

Uh-huh. Before the turn of the century. Even after we sold it, I had a great-great uncle that continued to manage it up until it was bought by the Moodys. They built the stone hotel that's there today. The original hotel was an old wooden building . . .

You used to go there as a child?

That's where I learned how to swim—when I was about two years old . . . My grandfather built the house on it . . . I moved here after school when I got married. I've been around the area all my life. We've owned the property . . . We spent every weekend down here. This was like our summer get-away. Mountain Lake was always a favorite trip . . .

Was it your great-grandfather who left a mark there?

He (great uncle) was the foreman of the Italian masons that built the house that is there today. And in the cornerstone of the building, I think he put a $5.00 gold piece or something like that in there.

NOTE: Per the Mountain Lake Hotel website: "The Porterfield family owned the lake for more than 30 years in the early 1900s and greatly refined the cuisine and hospitality."[12]

When *Dirty Dancing* was filming, were you strictly behind the scenes or were you in any of the scenes?

No, I was strictly behind the scenes. I fed them—that was my main contribution.

Well, I'd say that was a big one.

Well, it was an interesting one to say the least. We didn't have many guests there. That was fairly intentional because the movie people were paying us more really than having a place full of guests. There were some guests but September especially in those days was a very what we call shoulder season because at that time we closed at the end of October. We had very little business in September.

I thought I read somewhere that there was a bridge tournament over there?

That's a local event. Most people didn't stay there. They came up and played bridge.

In terms of feeding them, was there anything that you remember that stands out?

Most of the women went to a seafood shop in Blacksburg and bought their fish and brought it up and had us cook it. That in particular was Jennifer Grey, Cynthia Rhodes, someone else, who I can't remember . . . The rest of the people ate what we put out there.

A lot of diets?

It is show biz and I guess they did have to keep up their appearances in some fashion or another.

Well, the next one is a very big question. What was your contact with the cast and crew?

Believe it or not, they really didn't really want us around them very much. They were filming a movie. They didn't want us guys peaking around the corner and trying to see what was going on all the time naturally. So most of where they were filming was fairly well secluded to us.

I usually saw Buddy most every evening after dinner. He would come in and buy a six pack or two of beer. At that time, we only served beer and wine. We didn't have a liquor license. He used to amaze us because all beer we had for the most part was imported. The chef bought very nice imports. At that time, they sold for $2.00 a bottle. That was twelve bucks a six-pack which amazed us. Most of those kids I worked with were college kids. We bought Schaefer's and Old Milwaukee lights. We were amazed that somebody would spend that kind of money every night and invite us out and have some beers with us.

I'll tell you about Buddy. He came in the kitchen one night to get his beers. We had a dishwasher who had just recently gotten out of the Marines. This was a really weird little guy. The only way we could get him to work was to let him drink wine. He brought his own wine. We didn't provide it. We let him drink it 'cuz he would stay there and work. It was Maddog or Red Lady 21—one of those fortified wines. Buddy came back in there and was talking with him. He asked him, "Do you want a drink of beer?" and he said, "Sure," and had a big pull on the bottle. We just got a big kick out of that. Buddy was a really down-to-earth guy. He was not in the least bit pretentious. He would invite us out to the library to have beers with him. That's where I first spoke with Miranda [Garrison] when they were there filming the movie. She was a very nice lady.

On Friday evenings, we had a cookout . . . The chef was very close with his workers. We were almost like family 'cuz we worked together seven days a week per season. We became real close. We always worked the cookout, which Jerry Orbach came to, and sat and ate with us. He always sat at the table with the chef and his wife, who ran the dining room, that team there, myself, and the other cooks, and we ate together. Jack Weston ate with us.

This is a very rural county . . . Things are a little different when a big production comes to town and starts filming. I mean that place was covered with people all the time. They had state police up there to block the roads. All the locals wanted to come up there and see what was going on . . . It was a big thing. This is a pretty large county with a population just under seventeen thousand. There are four street lights in the whole county . . . It's a very rural area. We are twelve miles from Blacksburg, which is a huge metropolitan area for most people around here.

Is it Giles county?

Yes.

What about the motorcycle ride?

It was one evening. It was late and we were done with dinner, and we had cleaned up and were getting ready to leave. They had a crew that did nothing but drive from Blacksburg to Mountain Lake. It was a lucrative job to have. They paid $10.00 an hour. That was very good pay then to just drive people back and forth. They stopped that around seven o'clock in the evening and Buddy needed a ride to Blacksburg and came through and asked several people. Most of them all rode together and were way up on the other end of the county. So he got to the back dock, and I was up there, and he said, "Can you give me a ride?" I said, "Yep, can you ride on a motorcycle?" "Oh, that's no problem." He had the black leather jacket on. He was ready. I had an extra helmet much to the chagrin of my cousin, who also had a motorcycle but didn't have an extra helmet. So we loaded up on the bike and headed down the mountain. Now you've driven up the mountain; you know how curvy it is. When we got on the bike, he was holding on. It has a metal strap on the back and he was holding on to that. We started down the mountain and about the third curve, he grabbed me . . . and that's how he held on until we got to Blacksburg. When we got there, he was joking and we were laughing, and he said, "You can tell everybody you gave me a ride." I said, "No, you can tell everybody you rode down that mountain with me." The reason I said that was because my cousin and I were known to be very quick on our bikes.

Were they staying in a hotel there—some of them, some of the time?

Some of them. They didn't stay there all of the time but most of the time.

Kenny Ortega was there. Patrick Swayze did not stay there all the time.

For the most part, Patrick stayed at Mountain Lake. We did have rooms in Blacksburg if he wanted to go to town and hang out at the college town there. He ate dinner there at a restaurant that is very popular that I worked in . . . and everybody else worked in at one point in time. The name of the restaurant was Maxwells' . . . It was well known for its cuisine and that's what those people were used to if they wanted real good food. They also ate at Charlos.

I remember Matthew Broderick was dating Jennifer Grey then. He came there and he stayed for a couple of days with her. The little girls in the dining room were taking everything he touched—silver, saucer, coffee cup, anything he touched, they took.

What about Buddy?

You gotta remember these were all young kids. What they had just seen was *Ferris Bueller's Day Off*. They didn't pay a whole lot of attention to *Red Dawn*. They were just little girls. Patrick Swayze did attract a lot of attention there. He did without a doubt. There were a lot of people who definitely would want to see him, but all the younguns were more impressed with Matthew Broderick.

Anything else about Buddy?

He was just a real down-to-earth nice guy. I don't think a whole lot more needs to be said than that. He was very pleasant to be around. He didn't turn his nose up to you, which quite a few other people did. It is nice that he was that way. That is what people remember and appreciate.

What about anything else about any of the other people?

Well, other than talking with Buddy quite often, and Miranda, Jack Weston, Jerry Orbach.

Those were the only people . . .

Did you think the movie would be successful?

Quite frankly—no. I had no idea it would be as successful as it turned out to be.

Probably most people didn't—right?

Well, number one, although we know it is a feel-good movie—very popular these days—when I watched it, I kind of thought well you know that's a chick-flick. It's pretty well done. It's OK. I would probably watch Chuck Norris before I would watch *Dirty Dancing*. Granted, I did want to see it because I was just curious. It was nothing like what I imagined while they were filming. I even have one of the original scripts before they changed it to *Dirty Dancing*.

So why do you think *Dirty Dancing* is so popular?

That's a good question. Other than the fact it is a real feel-good movie— the guy gets the girl in the end. I really don't know. I didn't think it was going to happen. When it came out, it was popular there for awhile. It seems like it's been within the, I don't know, the past eight years, you see it on satellite TV on about four different channels all the time. I was impressed by this time. I was gone from Mountain Lake for awhile. I spent ten years there, and I left for ten years, and I've been back for eight. I really noticed the influx in the past eight years of people coming up there for *Dirty Dancing*.

An increase, more people . . .

It's really unreal to me. Buzz and I comment on that every time we're done with a tour. Can you believe that people are coming here for this thing? And it's a good thing for us.

Where do people come from? Which countries and states?

They seem to come from all over, from everywhere. I've talked to people there from Germany—who came there for that particular reason, and of course there's been a fair amount of people from the UK there. But people from all over the country. Our regular based guest is generally from Northern Virginia, Maryland area. That's our core of guests. I mean we have people from all over, but that is the main core. These people that are coming for the *Dirty Dancing* thing are from everywhere—Tennessee, North Carolina, Michigan . . . They're coming from everywhere.

There are stories . . . The leaves were spray painted green? That's true, isn't it?

Yes, indeed. There are rhododendron bushes all the way around there. They have a really dark green leaf and in the fall, they're turning brown and falling off. They came and spray painted them all green. They put a lot of cutsie stuff in there. They put little lanterns all over the place. They put in the little fence that we have there now. Awnings on the buildings. Fake rock was placed into the windows on the kitchen so you couldn't tell there were windows there. Just a lot of neat little stuff like that, which was beneficial to us too. Other than that, they were fairly unintrusive. It was weird just to be around there because they had these huge, big screens to direct the light this way and that . . . It was quite a production. When we didn't have business to do, we were out there watching this stuff. They would run us off when the filming began. You gotta remember we were the only guys who could come in there, as the police kept everybody else away.

What about those kerosene heaters?

They had kerosene heaters down under the tables (at the beach) because it was quite cold.

OK. So some guys were paid to have their '57 Chevies sit in the parking lot all day?

Uh-huh.

Do you know how much they were paid?

I only knew one person who actually had a vehicle out there . . . There were other people who did. There was one guy who lived there. He was a waiter and he had a '57 Chevy station wagon. You did not see it in the movie anywhere. But they did pay him. I think they gave him $20.00 a day, which was actually more than they gave to any of the extras.

What did the extras get?

$10.00 a day and lunch.

Note: Extras were expected to be available 12–14 hours a day per multiple sources.

They were all from Blacksburg?

All around . . . quite a large area, people from Beckley, West Virginia . . . lot of people from Roanoke. They were there from several surrounding areas.

That scene where it is pouring rain, and then Buddy breaks the car window so they can get in the car. So it really wasn't raining?

No.

I didn't know that. Honest to goodness.

They can do that stuff pretty well . . . we were watching . . . The hoses were on top of the porte cochere. That is the actual entrance to the hotel lobby. It is a covered drive thru—right off the dining room. Johnny was actually driving the wrong way as we use it today. So we were in the dining room just watching the whole thing.

What about other little stories?

I was in the kitchen when they filmed that scene. It was myself, with the chef and two other guys that worked there with us . . .

Baby and the nephew were going along there and they're opening the refrigerator and he says, "Well, what would you like? Some cabbage roll, some this and that, some lime sherbet?" Well, right there is where the chef's office is . . .

So we all said cut. And they stopped the whole thing and they actually weren't happy about it but they re-wrote it right then and there and changed it so he no longer says lime sherbet because it was a refrigerator—wasn't a freezer. That was our point. Plus, we were there for a reason. We had to cut off all the equipment in there. So we had to be in there to make sure nothing caught on fire or anything bad happened. Of course, we were in the chef's office and it is full of liquor. So we're imbibing a little bit. We had a few cocktails while we watched this transpire. They were filming at night because we had to cook in the morning. They had built fake walls in there, so it looked really black. We walked through the walls because we weren't used to walls being there. They probably weren't real happy by the time that night's filming was done, but what can you say.

So did you see it when Penny was kneeling on the floor?

Oh, yes.

She doesn't get a lot of attention.

Yeah, she doesn't but that corner does.

Well, I had my picture taken there. I admit it.

That's the most photographed place on Mountain Lake.

Are you serious?

I kid you not. Constantly, we're bringing people in there to have their picture taken. When we do the tour, we turn the lights down in that section of the kitchen. And I put one of my carbon lamps up on the line so it's pointing right down to where she would be hunkered down so everybody can get a picture just like it looked in the movie. That's just kind of neat. A lot of people enjoy that.

Buzz told me something about the guy who stepped on Jennifer's foot—like in the beginning of the movie when Penny was having them do the line dance.

Bobbie's dad. A real nice guy . . . He was in three shots so for three days' work he got $30.00. He has them all framed with a *Dirty Dancing* handbill in there. A real nice guy—loves to talk about his part in it.

Was the entire lift scene in the water done at Mountain Lake?

Yes.

What was it like to go to the premiere at The Lyric?

We all naturally wanted to see how that was going to go. Everybody who went was pretty excited about going. It was interesting. I thought they did a pretty good job of it. But I did not know that it would be what it is today.

Did they have the premier there the same time it was premiering around the country?

It was January or February . . .

So what do you think about the stage show? Have you seen it? If not, are you going to see it?

I've only seen the information that Buzz has brought back. It looks pretty interesting. If it gets a little closer, I probably will go see it. I would like to see it come really close by . . . I think it would help us a whole lot.

It would make sense to have it come close . . . wouldn't it? It's in Boston now, going to LA, and then maybe Broadway.

Actually, New York and Chicago are the closest.

So I think someone had to go buy stuff to put on the shelves in the kitchen to make it look like Kellerman's.

We had to get everything of ours off all shelves because they put their own props up there—matzah flour, gefilte fish. We did sneak some things in there.

What did you sneak in there?

There is a can of Old Bay sitting on the shelf. There's a set of ear plugs hanging where utensils would hang. I think A1. We were very mischievous in those days . . .

Do you have a favorite scene or a favorite character?

Naturally, my favorite scene is the kitchen part. That's just because I was there. It's one of the number one scenes as far as people want to see at Mountain Lake. They like to go down to Virginia Cottage and look around or they want to know what room Patrick Swayze stayed in and that corner in the kitchen . . .

So some of the people stayed at the hotel in Blacksburg. Was it a Marriott?

It was the Holiday Inn where you stayed in but at that time, it was a Marriott. Well, you know they had a lot of people. We just didn't have enough rooms. That's what it boiled down to.

That is really interesting. I never heard of that.
What about some of those other people—Eleanor Bergstein, Linda Gottlieb—sounds like you didn't see them too much.

Most I saw them around is when they were filming in the kitchen. 'Cuz they were all in there. You know us kitchen guys were pretty much in the kitchen all the time.

I don't know how many extras they had, but it sounds like you were cooking for a couple hundred people.

It was insane you see, because they would come in and say we need a walking dinner for three hundred people. Walking dinner means a sandwich—something you could pick up and walk away with. I didn't have ten–fifteen cases of anything in there. We didn't have three hundred hamburger patties. We were getting ready to close down in a month. We didn't have a lot of stuff here. The best I could do was make big batches of soup.

That sounds good. Nothing wrong with soup.

It was cold—that worked. But that was what I could do at that time. They catered a lot of pizza. They would go to Domino's and get a couple hundred pizzas. That made Domino's real happy . . . That was part of the deal—$10.00 and lunch for all the extras.

Would Buddy pay for the beer sometimes in the evenings?

He always paid for it . . . Of course, we didn't have $12.00 for a six pack. I think we were making five or six dollars an hour . . . it wasn't so glamorous. In those days, we had two days off. We worked from seven in the morning until closing at night. So we had breaks in between breakfast and lunch—and a big break between lunch and dinner— and we got to use all the facilities. During that time whenever they were filming, we tried to watch it.

It is so beautiful there. It is amazing.

It is a gorgeous place. I've been all over this world—literally. I am not prejudiced just because this is where I've been all my life. There is nothing that compares to it. It has four beautiful seasons and it's just a pretty part of the world. Virtually no crime.

MOUNTAIN LAKE PATRICK SWAYZE
MEMORIAL WEEKEND

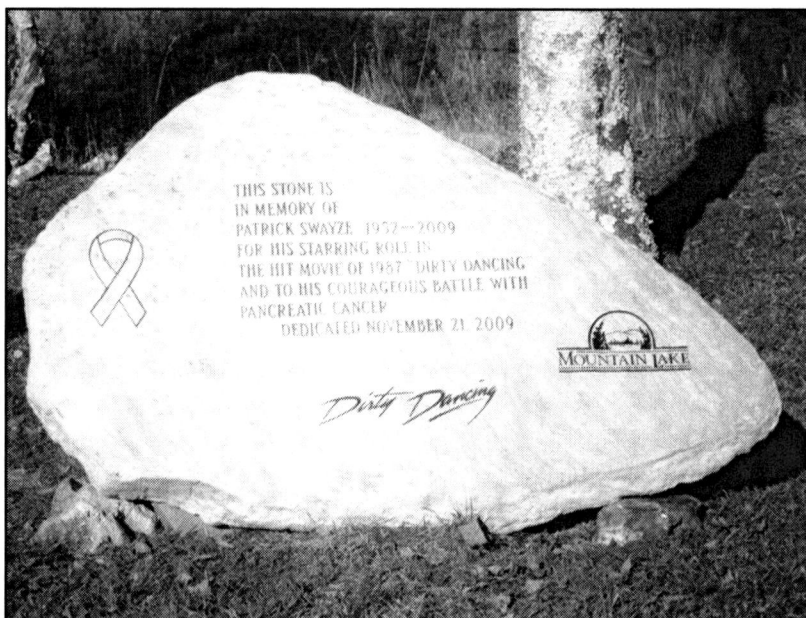

Credit: DJ Rick Pruett

Mountain Lake Hotel honored Mr. Swayze by holding The Patrick Swayze Memorial Weekend, November 20–22, 2009. On November 21, 2009, a dedication ceremony was held at the gazebo during which an engraved lift stone was dedicated to Mr. Patrick Swayze for his starring role in *Dirty Dancing* and his courageous battle with pancreatic cancer. The stone had been taken out of the lake at the hotel from the approximate location where the lift scene was filmed in 1986.

Mr. Buzz Scanland, General Manager at Mountain Lake Hotel, led the memorial ceremony. Ms. Abigail Bartley, Area Executive Director for The American Cancer Society, and Ms. Rita McClenny, Virginia Film Commissioner, also participated. Mr. Scanland and Ms. Bartley announced that Mountain Lake Hotel and The American Cancer Society are co-sponsoring a contest in which people contribute money for their guesses as to how many days it will take for the lake to re-fill. The donated money will be earmarked for pancreatic cancer research. The winner of the contest will get a stay for three nights at Mountain Lake Hotel.

DANCING FILM PRODUCTIONS, INC.

c/o Mountain Lake Hotel
Route 1, P.O. Box 105B
Pembroke, VA 24136
703/626-7251

MOUNTAIN LAKE GUEST LIST

1. Emile Ardolino
2. Linda Gottlieb
3. Eleanor Bergstein
4. Doro Bachrach
5. Curtis Pepper
6. Jennifer Grey
7. Patrick Swayze
8. Cynthia Rhodes
9. Jane Brucker - from 9/3
10. Jerry Orbach - from 9/3
11. Neal Jones - from 9/4
12. Lynne Lipton - from 9/4
13. Jack Weston - from 9/4
14. "Stan" - from 9/4 - approx. 9/5 (lv. 9/6)
15. Paula Truman - from 9/4 - approx. 9/11 (lv. 9/12)
16. Alvin Myerovich - from 9/4 - approx. 9/11 (lv. 9/12)
17. Antone Pagan - from 9/8 - approx. 9/9 (lv. 9/10)
18. Kelly Bishop - from 9/10 - approx. 9/12 (lv. 9/13)
19. Lonny Price - from 9/6
20. Adger Cowans - from 9/3
21. Mark Haack
22. ~~Jeffrey~~ Marilyn Bailes
23. Tom Allen
24. Hilary Rosenfeld
25. Claudia Anderson
26. Lisa Feldbauer
27. Mark Burchard
28. Steve Lineweaver
29. Kenny Ortega
30. Miranda Garrison
31. Julia Cort - from 9/3
32. Susan Pickett - from 9/2
33. Jennifer Gilbert
34. Mike Barrow
35. John Merriman - from 9/2 or 9/3
36. Quintin Woo - from 9/3
37. Scott Zigler - from 9/3
38. Greg White-Wiegand - 9/3
39. Donne Daniels
40. Peter Van Eynde - from 9/4
41. Bill Flick - from 9/3 or 9/4
42. Michael Sudmier - from 9/3 or 9/4
43. Marlies Vallant
44. Frida Aradottir
45. Jimi White
46. Jeanie D'Iorio
47. Isabelle Cramer
48. Sabrina Padwa

49. Jacob Conrad
50. Neil Holcomb

58

ame	1	2	3	4	5	6	7	8	9	10	11	12	13	14	15	16	17	18	19	Total
Ardolino, Emile 200	✓	✓	✓	✓	✓	✓	✓	✓	✓	✓	✓	✓		✓	217 ✓ 15	✓	✓		✓	1
Bergstien, Eleanor 218	✓	✓	✓	✓	✓	✓	✓	✓	✓	✓	✓	✓		✓	14			✓	✓	1
Gottlieb, Linda		103 ✓	113				310 ✓	✓	✓	✓		✓	✓		10		✓	✓		
Grey, Jennifer 303	✓	✓	✓	✓	✓	✓	✓	✓	✓	✓	✓	✓		✓	13 05	✓	✓	✓	✓	
Swayze, Patrick 232	✓	✓	✓	✓	✓	✓	314 ✓	✓	✓	✓	✓	✓	✓	✓	15			✓	✓	
weston, Jack	230 ✓	✓	✓	✓	✓	✓	314 ✓	✓	✓	✓	✓	✓		✓	15	✓	✓	✓	✓	
Orbach, Jerry 217	✓	✓	✓	✓	✓	✓	✓	✓	✓	✓	✓	✓		✓	14		310	✓	✓	
Bachrach, Doro 229	✓	✓	✓	✓	✓	✓	✓	✓	✓	✓	✓	✓	✓	✓	14		✓	✓	✓	
Rhodes, Cynthia 219	✓	✓	✓	✓	✓	✓	✓	✓	✓	✓	✓	✓	✓		14		207	✓	✓	
Truman, Paula				107 ✓	✓	✓	✓	✓	✓	✓	✓	✓	✓		11					
hyrovich, Alvin		See Gottleib		103 ✓	✓	✓	✓	✓	✓	✓	✓	✓	✓		11					
Price, Lonny								233 ✓	✓	✓	✓	✓	✓		1					
Lipton, Lynne		221 ✓	✓	✓	✓	✓	✓	✓	✓	See Bishop/Merriman					270					
Brucker, Jane 227	See Marshall/g	✓	✓	✓	✓	✓	✓	✓	✓	✓	✓	✓	✓	✓	107 13	✓	✓	✓	✓	
Jones, Neil 311	16 out	201 ✓	✓	✓	✓	✓	✓	✓	✓	✓	✓	✓		✓	12			✓	✓	
Feldbauer, Elizabeth	✓	✓	✓	✓	✓	✓	✓	✓	✓	✓	✓	✓	✓		14				✓	
Cramer, Isabelle 331	✓	✓	✓	✓	✓	✓			See Spencer									✓	✓	
Padwa, Sabrina 331	✓	✓	✓	✓	✓	✓	✓	✓	✓	✓	✓	✓	✓		14			✓	✓	
Allen, Tom	337 ✓	✓	✓	✓	✓	✓	✓	314 ✓	✓	✓	✓	✓	✓		14				✓	
Anderson, Claudia 325	✓	✓	✓	✓	✓	✓	✓	✓	✓	✓	✓	✓	✓		14					
Aradottir, Frida 309	✓	✓	✓	✓	✓	✓	✓	✓	✓	✓	✓	✓	✓		14		206	✓	✓	
Barrow, Mike	338 ✓	✓	✓	✓	✓	✓	✓	✓	✓	✓	✓	✓	✓		14			✓	✓	

DANCING FILM PRODUCTIONS, INC.

WELCOME!! Thank you for coming to our open call. We are casting for extras to be in the movie DANCING! which is shooting in the Blacksburg area September 5-19, 1986.

DANCING! starring Patrick(The Outsiders)Swayze and Jennifer(Ferris Bueller's Day Off)Grey, is the story of a young girl's summer in the Catskills in 1963 in a glamourous family resort where she falls in love with a handsome young dance instructor from "the other side of the tracks," learns to dance, and grows into a responsible and mature young woman.

If you are chosen to be in our movie, you can expect a phone call sometime within the next week or two. You will be expected to provide your own transportation to and from the location. You will be paid a small stipend per day, and fed lunch.

In filling out our questionnaire, please give as many telephone numbers as you can, including friends, neighbors, parents, and workplaces where we might be able to leave a message. The easier you are to reach, the better chance you have of being in the movie. Please include the best times to be reached at these numbers.

Also indicate your general schedule, and if it is flexible. This way if we need somebody at the last minute, we'll know who to call.

If you accept a job as an extra, there are a few things you should know about the "job."

1. Filming starts early and runs long -- generally <u>12-14 hours</u> -- so do not accept a call as an extra unless your whole day is free.

2. If you cannot make the day or days you are scheduled for, please give us a call, otherwise we will be counting on you. DO NOT send your husband, wife, or neighbor instead -- you've been chosen for a specific scene for a reason.

3. If you are called for a wardrobe fitting, please bring the items you have listed on the wardrobe list to the fitting with you. Remember, this is 1963, not the 80's, so don't check those items unless they seem period (think Jackie Kennedy and Sandra Dee). MEN: You will need to get your hair cut, so be prepared for that.

4. You will be asked to call us the afternoon or the evening before you work (that's when we tell you the specifics of where to report and at what time). If our lines are busy, please keep trying, as we are talking to alot of people!

5. Again, thank you for coming, and as soon as you've filled out the questionnaire completely, please get in line to have your picture taken.

Thank you, and we look forward to working with you!!

Four

OTHER FILM LOCATIONS

LAKE LURE INN

The second film location for *Dirty Dancing* was at Lake Lure Inn in Lake Lure, North Carolina. Filming at this 1927 recently restored inn and spa occurred from September 20 to October 27, 1986. The wrap party actually occurred right here also. Even though a fire about fifteen years ago destroyed some of the landmarks from the film, guests may still stay in the rooms where Mr. Swayze and Ms. Grey stayed while filming.

Scenes that were filmed at Lake Lure Inn include: the interior dance scenes (including the grand finale), the scene in which Johnny and Baby practice dancing on a log, Johnny's cabin scene, Baby on the rock stairway, and the employee cottages scenes. There are several famous stories regarding some of these scenes. Mr. Swayze (who refused a stuntman) while teaching "Baby" fell off the log several times and had to be taken to the hospital to have his knee drained, and then was back to work the very next day. Ms. Grey was stung by wasps several times while filming the famous Johnny's cabin scene.

RUMBLING BALD RESORT

The golf course scene was filmed at Rumbling Bald resort on Lake Lure at Hole 16. This scene is when Baby's parents were putting and Baby asked her dad for money.

Rumbling Bald Resort is located in North Carolina near Charlotte, Greenville, and Asheville—on the north side of Lake Lure.

I had the absolute pleasure of interviewing Mr. Gary Wilson from Rumbling Bald Resort regarding the filming of the golf course scene.

GARY WILSON

Age 60. Lives in North Carolina.

March 2009 (telephone and e-mail interviews).

What is your position at Rumbling Bald Resort, and how long have you worked there?

Head of Security. I have worked there since December 1971. We got to see some of the filming . . . I met Patrick Swayze. He was a nice guy.

Gary told me that Patrick was the only one of the leads that he spoke to. Even though Patrick was not in the golf course scene, Gary had contact with him.

Patrick came over a couple of times. I let him through the gate. He was there during part of the filming and also came with other people for lunch one day.

How long did the filming take?

The scene at the golf course was shot in a couple of days—one entire day and part of another day.

How far away is Rumbling Bald Resort from Lake Lure Inn?

Lake Lure Inn is at the other side of the lake and is about fifteen minutes away.

Did you think *Dirty Dancing* would be popular?

I never thought it would be that popular. We still get fans asking to see the golf course.

Gary confirmed that there is a plaque at Hole 16 commemorating where Dirty Dancing *was filmed. Also, he indicated that the fans are allowed to walk with the walking club at specified times if they want to see the hole.*

Why do you think that *Dirty Dancing* has remained so popular?

I think the movie's songs, dance themes, and characters reflect a simpler time that so many of us remember from our youth. For the younger generation who like it—my youngest daughter who was barely born when it came out and who has probably watched it thirty times! likes the simplicity of it without all the complicated, sordid story lines that are present in today's movies and in today's life.

Do you have a favorite scene or character in the movie?

Patrick Swayze was my favorite. I have always liked him. He seems to be a genuinely nice guy. Hope his health improves. He's a fighter. My favorite scene was the dance scene at the end with "Baby."

Gary also told me that the fire at Lake Lure Inn in which the main building burned down was about fifteen years ago. The property was bought and sold.

Also, he informed me that the movie, *Last of the Mohicans* was filmed at Rumbling Bald Resort.

Still taken from *Dirty Dancing*.
Credit: Vestron/Kobal Collection

This moment is probably one of the most important in the entire film. Johnny (Patrick Swayze) has returned to Kellerman's (after he had been asked to leave quietly), and takes Baby out of the corner, and up to the microphone. He says he is going to do the last dance his way—with Ms. Frances Houseman (Baby—Jennifer Grey). Johnny stands up for Baby and himself, and thus shows his respect for Baby, himself, and their relationship—in spite of what other people may think.

Still taken from *Dirty Dancing*.
Credit: Vestron/Kobal Collection

Johnny (Patrick Swayze) and Baby (Jennifer Grey) dance in the finale scene of the movie. Their eyes reflect their heart and soul connection.

Steve Schwartz and one of his dance partners, Nadine Leach, in 1956 in Miami Beach. This picture was the poster for the Mambo Jamboree that he ran at the De Lido Hotel. Steve Schwartz—also known by his professional dancer name Steve Sands—was the dance partner of Jackie Horner (consultant to Eleanor Bergstein) at Grossinger's in the '50s. Per Jackie Horner, "He's the Johnny (Patrick Swayze)."

Mr. H. M. "Buzz" Scanland Jr., General Manager at Mountain Lake Hotel, was a very gracious host to me during my visit there in January 2009. This shot was taken in the dining room looking out at the beautiful Mountain Lake property. Buzz was the marketing manager when *Dirty Dancing* was filming there in 1986.

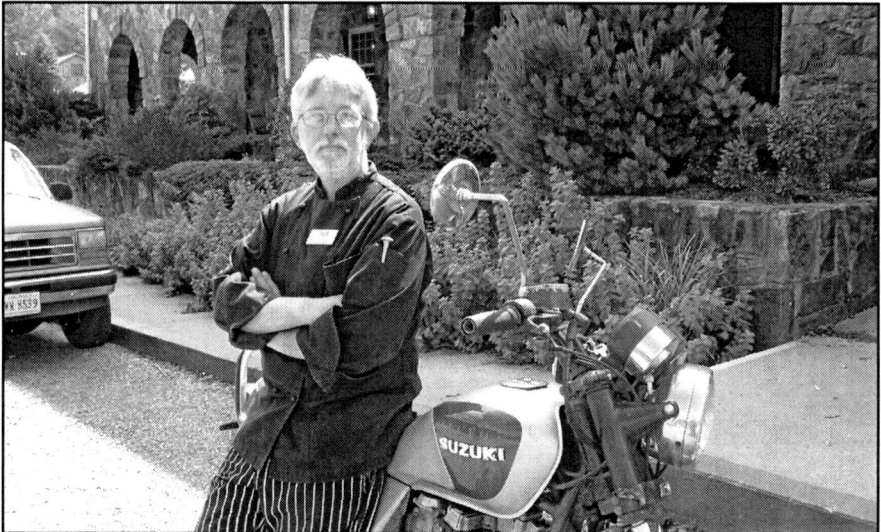

Mr. Mike Porterfield, Executive Chef at Mountain Lake Hotel, is standing in front of the hotel. He gave Patrick Swayze a ride on his motorcycle down the mountain when *Dirty Dancing* was filming there, and was one of the people who hung out with Patrick Swayze, Miranda Garrison, and others in the evenings. Mike's family used to own the property—beginning in the late 1880s for more than thirty years.

Swayze Mania Ladies on their reunion trip in the dining room at Mountain Lake Hotel with the popular cardboard Patrick Swayze. Per Roberta Teska (first fan standing on left side): "While we were having our first dinner in the dining room (with 'Patrick' at the head of the table), we had lots of fun . . . Our Swayze Mania friend and husband arrived and went up to the front desk and asked where they could find us. The clerk said, 'They're in the dining room having dinner with Patrick!'

Roberta also shared, "Two of the Swayze Mania ladies were lucky enough to share Room 232, which was Patrick's room when he was at Mountain Lake Hotel filming *Dirty Dancing* . . . I asked Buzz, the manager, 'Why don't you have a plaque up on the door stating this fact?' He replied, 'It wouldn't even last a day.'"

Scenes at this famous Mountain Lake gazebo include: Baby (Jennifer Grey) had her foot stepped on by a male guest during a dance class, Johnny (Patrick Swayze) was dancing with various guests and then alerted that Penny (Cynthia Rhodes) was in need of help, and Dr. Houseman (Jerry Orbach) and Baby had their father/daughter talk here.

Credit: Sue Tabashnik

Here is another shot of the Mountain Lake dining room where Johnny (Patrick Swayze) told Robbie (Max Cantor), the college boy, where to put the pickle. Also, this is where the Housemans had their first dinner, and the breakfast when Dr. Houseman (Jerry Orbach) talked about leaving early.

Credit: Buzz Scanland

Buzz took my picture in this famous kitchen where Penny (Cynthia Rhodes) crouched down crying, and soon Johnny (Patrick Swayze) arrived on the scene to rescue her. Per Mike Porterfield, this is one of the most popular places for fans at Mountain Lake Hotel to have their picture taken.

Credit: Sue Tabashnik

Buzz is braving the six below zero temperature to show the beautiful wintry Mountain Lake Hotel property.

Rachael Harrell and Maury Denton. Richmond, Virginia. "We visited Mountain Lake to celebrate our love and our love for dancing. Like Johnny and Baby, we met on a dance floor. Thank you to our friends, Warren and Emily Bailey, for helping us re-create the lift that captured the hearts of romantics around the world."

Emily Bailey lives with her husband, Warren and son in Chesterfield, Virginia. Emily is standing on the porch of the Houseman Cottage (now-a-days known as the Virginia Cottage) looking out at Mountain Lake. "My wife is truly a gift from God that I don't appreciate near enough. So for our four year anniversary, I was trying to do something really special. While reading *Virginia Wine Lover* magazine, I found out that *Dirty Dancing*, her all-time favorite movie, was filmed at Mountain Lake Hotel in Pembroke, VA. I further found out that our anniversary fell on one of the *Dirty Dancing* weekends. I told her to pack up for a weekend getaway and we drove our motorcycles the 4.5 hour trip. We pulled up in front of the hotel, and when she realized where we were, she was beside herself. It was an anniversary to remember!"

Five

INTERVIEWS OF THE FANS

ELLY ALI

Age 17. Lives in Melbourne, Australia.

July 2008 (e-mail interview).

Has seen *Dirty Dancing* over 500 times.

> **What year did you first see *Dirty Dancing*? How old were you? Did someone tell you about the movie or did you just happen to hear about it? Did you initially watch it by yourself or with someone else?**

I first ever saw *Dirty Dancing* in the year 2005. I was fourteen years old. I had heard about *Dirty Dancing* through my parents. They would talk about how popular it was back in their time in the '80s. My mum told me she went to see it at the movies when she was a teenager, and she said she really loved it. She said it was one of those movies that you would love to watch over and over again because of its great music, dancing, and acting. My dad had also told me a lot about it and how popular it was in the '80s, especially the music which is still played and heard by many people today—including myself. So one day I went out shopping and I couldn't wait to get my hands on my very own copy of *Dirty Dancing*. I initially watched *Dirty Dancing* with my dad. It was a Saturday night, and we put it on, and we had the time of our life watching it.

Why do you like *Dirty Dancing* so much?

I love *Dirty Dancing* so much because it's a movie that has so much meaning, and it has great actors and dancers and music in it. I especially love how Patrick Swayze and Jennifer Grey can work together in such a natural, sexy, and trusting way. I have always been a big fan of Patrick Swayze, ever since I was a little girl, and I have always loved to sing and dance. When I watched *Dirty Dancing, the* whole movie blew me away, and it made me realize that I can get out there and do what I love and what I have a big passion for, and not let anyone or anything stop me. I have learned never to be put in a corner and stand up for what I truly believe in, no matter what it costs me.

How has *Dirty Dancing* impacted you personally?
You mentioned on the questionnaire that:

I can relate to the movie in so many ways, such as being seventeen and breaking away and individuating in your own unique way. Me and Jennifer Grey are alike, and I really look up to her in a way that she has given me the strength and power to stand up for myself and stand up for what I truly believe in, no matter if it's to dance or to fall in love. I really thank her for that. Patrick is a dream come true. They could not have picked better actors to suit this film. Those two have a great chemistry which nobody can take away from them. It will live on forever because nobody puts Baby and Johnny in a corner.

Anything else you want to say about the above?

No, that covers it.

I think that you mentioned that you want to be a singer and dancer. How has *Dirty Dancing* influenced you in that regard, and are you actively pursuing a career as a singer/dancer?

Dirty Dancing has influenced me to get out there and have confidence, pride, and passion to do what I love to do best, and don't let anything get in my way or don't let anything stop me from living my dreams and finding happiness. I am currently looking into finding the right place for me—a dance studio, singing lessons.

I want to follow my heart. After all, *Dirty Dancing* is exactly why I started to dance in the first place. It's my passion and long-term commitment.

Are there other ways the movie has impacted you?

Yes, there are other ways the movie has impacted me and they are: stand up for what you believe in no matter what it costs you. Don't let anyone put you in a corner. Things are not as perfect as they seem—trust, honesty. Believe in yourself and don't let others weigh you down and make you feel like you are worthless or treat you like you are nothing.

In addition *to Dirty Dancing*, how many movies have you seen multiple times? If there are other movies that you have seen multiple times, is Patrick in them?

I have seen multiple movies which definitely feature Patrick Swayze in them. They are: *One Last Dance* (at least twenty times), *Ghost* & *Road House* (watch both all of the time), *The Outsiders*, *Red Dawn*, *Dirty Dancing: Havana Nights*, and *Father Hood*. I own all of Patrick's movies and love all of them. *One Last Dance* is the most touching film I have ever seen.

Have you ever met Patrick Swayze or anyone else from the cast? If so, what was it like?

No, I have never met Patrick Swayze or anyone else from the cast. I wish I could say yes, but that would be lying. I would love one day to meet Patrick Swayze and I never say never because things happen when you least expect them to. It would be a dream come true if I ever met Patrick Swayze or cast from the film.

Will you continue to watch *Dirty Dancing*?

Yes, I will indeed continue to watch *Dirty Dancing*. No matter how many times I have already seen it over the previous years, I will always love *Dirty Dancing,* and I still to this day continue to watch it. I have even learned all the dance routines. I know the script from start to finish, and I constantly listen to the soundtrack over and over again, especially "(I've Had) The Time Of My Life," "She's Like The Wind," "Hungry Eyes," "Cry to Me," "Be My Baby," "Yes," "Overload," "Hey Baby," "Do You Love Me," and "Some Kind of Wonderful." I love all the tracks, but they are my top nine that I repeat over and over.

What do you think about *Dirty Dancing*, the movie being made into the stage production, and do you plan to see the stage production?

I think *Dirty Dancing,* the movie, would be a great stage production. I would definitely plan to go and see it on stage, but I will not feel as passionate about the play as I feel about the movie unless the actual cast from the film was to do the stage production.

Do you think a sequel could be made?

It's hard to tell. I recently saw *Dirty Dancing: Havana Nights*. I can't say that I disliked the film but as soon as I saw that Patrick Swayze made a cameo appearance, I enjoyed it even more. It just cannot be compared to the first *Dirty Dancing*—a film that many people from all over the world saw, a film that everybody talked about, a film that became a phenomenon, and just could not be replaced or be compared to films in today's generation that have story lines that are rare and seem almost impossible.

Seeing Patrick in *Dirty Dancing: Havana Nights* made me want to see the movie to see the scenes that he is in. He still remains the hotel dance instructor but this time in Havana, Cuba not at Kellerman's. He still teaches ladies how to dance. He shows great interest and helps Katie overcome her fear towards her feelings of her connection towards her dance partner, Javier and how she moves. If I compare this to the 1987 *Dirty Dancing*, he helps Baby overcome her fear of the lift. He makes her find trust in him and they fall in love despite what her family thinks. *Dirty Dancing: Havana Nights* however shows Katie does find that trust in Javier, and they fall in love even though her parents forbid her. I still don't feel that connection towards this adaptation as I did for Jennifer Grey and Patrick Swayze. They made this movie one that nobody could ever forget. I'm only seventeen years old, and I strongly feel that the way Patrick and Jennifer worked together with such great teamwork and sharing a soul level connection in this movie—nobody could ever fill that gap because if those two were not as great as they were, nobody can ever be better or think they were better. They were just brilliant, and they made it so natural and they made it seem so real.

I would definitely love to see the whole cast together again. It would be fantastic to see Baby and Johnny together aging after soooooooo many years, with a few surprises added in, such as Penny has a baby, Lisa and Billy are involved in a relationship, and everyone is happy and changed, but *Dirty Dancing* never faded—it's still alive . . . just to see the two of them—Patrick and Jennifer—together again as they make such an amazing couple.

Do you know anyone else around your age who watches *Dirty Dancing?*

Yes, my best friend, other friends, and I have cousins who watch it but they are not as passionate and obsessed as I am about the film, and especially about Patrick Swayze.

Is there anything else you want to say about *Dirty Dancing?*

Dirty Dancing is by far my favorite movie and it reminds me of this time in my life, being seventeen and seeing life through my own eyes.

I own two versions of the film. I have just the DVD (on its own) and I recently bought the 20th Anniversary Edition. I couldn't help myself. I just had to buy it. I bought it because it features never before seen deleted scenes, alternate scenes and extended scenes, cast interviews, music videos, *Dirty Dancing* with Patrick Swayze (my favorite by far), multi-angle dance sequence, outtakes and screen tests, trivia track, and much more.

I just can't get enough of *Dirty Dancing*. I really appreciate Eleanor Bergstein, Emile Ardolino, Kenny Ortega and everybody else who made the movie possible. Wonderful, Fantastic, Brilliant, and Entertaining. It has been an exhilarating experience.

Additional Demographic Information

Marital status: Single

Occupation/Profession: Student, singer, dancer, administration worker

Official Patrick Swayze International Fan Club member: No

HELENA DAMIGOU

AGE 24. Lives in Athens, Greece.

December 2008 (e-mail interview).

Has seen *Dirty Dancing* 51–100 times.

What year did you first see *Dirty Dancing*? And how old were you?

It was the year of 1996. I was about twelve years old. I remember it as if it were yesterday. My parents had plans for the night and were going out with some friends. I was supposed to stay home with my older brother and I made plans of my own. I would sit in front of the TV, eat my homemade popcorn and relax. The moment I turned on the TV, I saw a movie that was about to start and it instantly attracted me. I loved the song that it was playing in the beginning. I loved the characters, the plot, Patrick Swayze and Jennifer Grey. It seemed like something was keeping me on that couch, a feeling I had never felt before. From that day on, I fell in love with *Dirty Dancing*.

Why do you like *Dirty Dancing* so much?

Dirty Dancing, in my opinion, is the ultimate love story—a story about two people that the chances of them ever meeting were very few. But they did meet, fell in love against all odds and protected that love with their hearts and souls. Became better persons along the way and realized that love is worth giving, as well as losing everything. I had seen many movies that talked about love stories, great passions, unspeakable romances but this movie has heart. It has rhythm, it has spirit. It moves you in a way few things do in this life. But the best thing about this movie is that you see this love as it grows, as it flourishes, and you become a part of it—you feel like you are part of it.

How has *Dirty Dancing* impacted you personally?

The reason that makes people watch movies has a deeper meaning than just plain old entertainment. It's a way to escape from our daily problems, a way to experience emotions or situations that every day life rarely gives you the chance to. Every person finds something in the kind of movies he likes that is missing from his own life, or that he would like to have lived. *Dirty Dancing* is the kind of movie I like because it gives me the opportunity to witness a love so strong and so overwhelming—like the one I have always dreamt of having. It's really the realization of the fairytale with the prince on his white horse that comes and takes me away and we live happily ever after, only in a more "up-to-date" kind of way. Many people, including myself, have lost faith in these kinds of romances and love stories because they seem so unreal, almost like fairytales. But this movie really makes me believe that there is still hope for every person in this world to find the love of their life, and no matter what the obstacles are, to have the chance to let themselves get carried away. It's really a lighthouse of hope that is shimmering in our hearts and that is keeping our faith in love strong and everlasting.

In addition to *Dirty Dancing*, what are names of movies that you have seen multiple times, and is Patrick in them?

The movies I have seen multiple times are: *Ghost*, with Patrick Swayze and Demi Moore; *Frankie and Johnny*, with Michelle Pfeiffer and Al Pacino; *Pretty Woman*, with Julia Roberts and Richard Gere; *Steel Magnolias*, with Shirley MacLaine, Dolly Parton, Daryl Hannah, Olympia Dukakis, and Julia Roberts; *What Dreams May Come*, with Robin Williams, Annabella Sciorra, and Cuba Gooding Jr.; *The Lake House*, with Sandra Bullock and Keanu Reeves, and last but not least *Beyond Borders*, with Angelina Jolie and Clive Owen. Actually, I can go on and on because I love movies, but these are the ones I have seen so many times I lost count. I have seen other movies with Patrick, but I haven't seen them with the same frequency as *Dirty Dancing*.

Have you ever met Patrick or anyone from the cast? If so, what was it like?

No, I haven't had the honor to meet any one of them.

Will you continue to watch *Dirty Dancing*?

Of course, I will continue to watch *Dirty Dancing* because it keeps that feeling alive and it's also a lovely movie to see over and over again.

What do you think about *Dirty Dancing*, the movie being made into a stage production, and do you plan on seeing it?

I honestly don't know how it would be like if the movie were to be made in the stage production because of the lack of sceneries that are really a big part of the movie and very important in the plot. I would surely go and see it because it's still a challenge to anyone who would have taken the risk to make DD a stage production, and it would be something interesting to see.

Do you think a good sequel to the movie could be made?

There is a sequel to the movie as I have seen in the video stores, called "*Dirty Dancing*: Havana Nights." I haven't seen it yet but I believe, without criticism, that there can only be one *Dirty Dancing* with that passion, that music, those actors, that greatness this movie brings out. I don't think that anyone, no matter how hard he would try, could duplicate this movie.

Do you think *Dirty Dancing* is popular in Greece?

DD is very popular in Greece, even though I had my doubts at first as far as how many people would know about this movie here. But after I had discussed it with a bunch of friends and relatives, I discovered that not only they knew about it and had seen it, but they also like it very much.

Anything else you want to say about *Dirty Dancing*?

Words are never enough when I want to express my feelings about this once-in-a-lifetime movie. The only thing I can add is that the memory of this epic love story keeps me warm in the heart and draws a smile on my face when I go to bed at night . . . it's really my favorite fairytale . . .

Additional Demographic Information

Marital status: Single

Education level: University

Occupation: Insurance advisor

Official Patrick Swayze International Fan Club member: No

CLARE GREGAN

Age 26. Lives in Preston, England.

January 2008 & November 2008 (e-mail interviews).

Has seen *Dirty Dancing* over 500 times.

Why do you like *Dirty Dancing* so much?

I feel the film is inspiring, a feel-good film with a great love story to tell. I think the music, dancing, and most of all the actors who played the parts were well suited. It always leaves you with a smile on your face, a warm heart, and a hope we'll all meet our Johnny Castle one day!

How has *Dirty Dancing* impacted you?

I think the film shows you that we are all different people from different backgrounds. However, at the same time, we can all learn something from one another and more so you learn from the film that sometimes you think you know someone or have an idea of the sort of person they are, when in reality you don't know that person at all. People can sometimes make themselves come across as something they are not in order to protect themselves. I think it teaches and makes you realize never to judge people without knowing them.

Also, see answer to question: Have you ever met Patrick or anyone from the cast?

In addition to *Dirty Dancing*, what movies have you seen multiple times? And is Patrick in them?

ICON	10–15 times
GHOST	80–100 times
KEEPING MUM	30 times
TO WONG FOO	15–20 times

(Patrick is in all of the above movies.)

Have you ever met Patrick or anyone else from the cast?

When I was a six year old girl at home one rainy weekend, my mother's friend came round with a video for them to watch. I was told it was a little too old for me to watch but being the nosey six year old I was at the time, I didn't give up and sat and watched the film with them. It was that rainy Saturday that I fell in lust with the one and only . . . Mr. Swayze! After that day and up until this day, I think I have seen the film nearer to 600 times and I'm now 26. I know the whole script—word for word! Dare I admit it! So from that Saturday, I was always found sitting watching *Dirty Dancing* and I made a promise to my dad that "When I'm a big girl, I'm going to America to find and hunt Patrick down!" That promise I always made sure everyone, including my dad, heard on a day-to-day basis.

My dad used to come home with the huge posters of him from the music store . . . Crazy things that mean so much when you are growing up and have an idol! Since then, I have seen every film that Patrick has filmed, joined the fan club, and most importantly that dream that the little six year old girl had those years ago came true in 2006 when I met the man who I grew up adoring and admiring.

It started on August 5th Saturday 2006. I was going to London with my mother and stepfather to watch the West End production of *Guys and Dolls* that Patrick was starring in. I'd seen the advertisement on his website and knew that was my chance of making that little girl's dream come true. So, I booked the ticket and we set off from Preston Lancashire to London. As soon as he came on stage, I was totally amazed, shocked, couldn't believe he was there a few feet away from me. The show was amazing but that wasn't enough. After the show, we raced round to the stage door where we waited for an hour and there he was standing right in front of me talking to the crowd, all to be over too soon, and I never got my chance to say a few words to him face-to-face. Heading back to Lancashire, I was still in shock that I'd seen the man I had idolized for the last nineteen years, but I still wasn't satisfied. So, I went back, with my friend. I drove all the way back—the 300 miles, got there early to the stage door to wait for Patrick to arrive, but he was held up in a traffic jam on the way to the theatre. I was informed by his bodyguard that he would be rushing back to go on stage, so we had to go and take our places inside, but he would get Patrick to sign my program for me.

Inside we watched the show and came out early before it finished, to get back to the stage door to get my front row position to see Patrick—when he came out to chat to the crowd, as he did after every production. Once again, I was talking to the bodyguard. He was very friendly and agreed to get my book signed by the man himself.

Patrick again came out to talk to the crowd and I was standing at the front. I waved my hand in his direction and he came over and shook my hand. He spoke to me—asked my name. Amazing! I had done it. Patrick then went back through the gates and people were starting to leave. I stood there with my friend upset that the bodyguard had not done as he'd said and gotten my program signed. So upset and deciding where to go next, his bodyguard came over to me, and said he needed a word with me. I was so very worried as to what maybe I had done wrong. I stepped forward to be taken through the electric gates to the stage door. As they opened—standing right in front of me was Patrick Swayze—looking right back at me, Clare Gregan, the girl with a dream from nineteen years ago . . . So you see, dreams really do come true.

That is just an insight into my story. I went on to date Patrick's bodyguard, met Patrick, and spent time and shared several more occasions with himself and his lovely wife, Lisa and cast and crew of the production.

I wanted to tell my story. As silly as it is probably to some people, that was my dream, and I had made a promise that one day I would meet my idol . . . Although it didn't take me to America that time to hunt him down (guess he saved me a flight fare), I got there in the end, and that was the best three months of my life.

It all started back one rainy Saturday afternoon with a six year old girl. And now my four year old little boy is amazed by the film. He knows all of the words to "(I've Had) the Time of My Life" and is planning on following in Patrick's footsteps. The film means so much to some people.

I hope you don't mind me sharing my dream with you . . .

Will you continue to watch *Dirty Dancing*?

With my little boy now taking over my obsession with the film, having me do the last dance routine with him in my front room, I think I'll be watching the film for some years to come yet!

What do you think about *Dirty Dancing*, the movie being made into a stage production, and do you plan on seeing the stage production?

Honestly, I think it was more money making than anything . . . I also feel that you cannot make such a fantastic film into a stage production and get from it so much like you do from the film. Therefore, I would not choose to go and watch the live performance.

Do you think a sequel could be made?

I think the film should remain as a one and only. People have their own view as to how Johnny and Baby went on from "The Last Dance." The film was a heartfelt and general feel-good factor. I think a second would only ruin the memory of *Dirty Dancing*. Sequels are never good and with such a special film that put Patrick on the front line internationally, I think it would be disrespectful, and with only a slight few of the original cast alive, I just couldn't see it working.

Additional Demographic Information

Marital status: With partner

Education: Graduated from Wellfield High, England, July 1998

Occupation/profession: Personnel Administrator

Official Patrick Swayze International Fan Club member: Joined in 2005

LELIA BAKO

Age 30. Lives in Resita, Romania.

March 2008 (e-mail interview).

Has seen *Dirty Dancing* 2–15 times.

What year did you first see *Dirty Dancing*, and how old were you?

First time I was sixteen years old. Now I have thirty years.

Why do you like *Dirty Dancing* so much?

I love the music, the actors . . . [since] the first time, I like Patrick and I think he is just great, a big actor.

How has *Dirty Dancing* impacted you personally?

When I first see this movie, my dream was to learn to dance.

In addition to *Dirty Dancing*, how many movies have you seen multiple times? If there are movies that you have seen multiple times, is Patrick in them?

Another film that moves me is *Titanic*.

Have you ever met Patrick or anyone else from the cast?

No, and I regret this.

Will you continue to watch *Dirty Dancing*?

Yes, I love this movie and when I am feeling lonely, I just love to stay in bed and enjoy this wonderful film.

What do you think about *Dirty Dancing*, the movie being made into the stage production? Do you plan to see the stage production?

I think this is a great idea. Yes, I hope to see this stage production.

Do you think *Dirty Dancing* is popular with many people in Romania?

Yes, it is very popular, especially between females of 20–50 years.

Additional Demographic Information

Education: College

Occupation/profession: Middle management

Official Patrick Swayze International Fan Club member: No

SIMONE GRADL

Age 32. Lives in Amberg, Germany.

April 2008 (e-mail interview).

Has seen *Dirty Dancing* 101–500 times.

What year did you first see *Dirty Dancing*, and how old were you?

1988. Twelve years old.

Why do you like *Dirty Dancing* so much?

 . . . With the film everything [goes together]. The music, dances, actor[s], history.

How has *Dirty Dancing* impacted you personally? On the questionnaire, you checked off, "has given hope that love exists and people will do the right thing," and "has provided relief in a difficult time. "Anything else you would like to say about this?

Applies exactly to me.

In addition to *Dirty Dancing*, how many movies have you seen multiple times? And is Patrick in them?

Have *One Last Dance, Ghost, North and South, Icon* and have watched many times. I love all films of Patrick.

Have you ever met Patrick or anyone else from the cast?

Met Patrick and Lisa on 29 July, 2006 in London [when Patrick was in *Guys and Dolls*].

 Will you continue to watch *Dirty Dancing*?

One can never get enough of the film.

What do you think about *Dirty Dancing*, the movie being made into the stage production? Do you plan to see the stage production?

I find it beautiful that the film will be on stage.

Do you think *Dirty Dancing* is very popular in Germany?

I think *Dirty Dancing* is popular in Germany.

I find it sad that the twenty year anniversary was so largely celebrated [in the]US.

Anything else you want to say about *Dirty Dancing*?

Dirty Dancing is part of my life.

Additional Demographic Information

Marital status: Live [s] with boyfriend

Education: Hauswirtschaftlerin

Occupation/profession: Work [s] in hospital kitchen

Official Patrick Swayze International Fan Club member: Joined September 1998

ANGELA GRUBB

AGE 34. Lives in Sumter, South Carolina.

April 2008 (e-mail and telephone interviews).

Has seen *Dirty Dancing* over 500 times.

What year did you first see *Dirty Dancing*? And how old were you?

I saw *Dirty Dancing* in 1987. I was fourteen years old.

Why do you like *Dirty Dancing* so much?

Where do I start? The main reason being Patrick starred in it. The coming of age story was fantastic and very believable. It made me think that maybe I could have something like that when I got little older. I also loved the dancing! I can't dance that way, but I would love for Patrick to teach me. LOL.

How has *Dirty Dancing* impacted you personally? I know that you made some wonderful comments on the questionnaire.

Watching *Dirty Dancing* gave me an "escape" from life as I was growing up. I had a difficult childhood and when I would turn on the VCR, I instantly stepped into Johnny & Baby's world. It kept me together.

I was wondering if there was anything else that you wanted to add or re-iterate, and why was it *Dirty Dancing* that you chose?

I was already in love with Patrick "The Actor" because of his role as "Orry Maine" in *North and South, Love and War*. I was excited to see him in a new movie. Then when I watched it for the first time, I just got lost in the love story. I loved how Patrick and Jennifer danced.

Going back to what I touched on in my questionnaire, I felt so alone and for some reason when I watched *Dirty Dancing*, it made me feel better. I guess I was grasping for the fact that some day that could be me, when I found my first true love. I had lots of bad days so I wound up watching

DD several times a week, to almost daily at times. I used to be able to tell you exactly where certain scenes were using the counter on the VCR. My best friend, Amy and I would watch DD and imitate the dances. We knew word for word a lot of the scenes. It seems silly to say that a movie made that much of an impact on me and my life, but it truly did. What is amazing is that it wasn't just me who fell in love with the story.

In addition to *Dirty Dancing*, how many movies have you seen multiple times? And is Patrick in them?

Let's see . . . The ones with Patrick that I can think of off the top of my head are: *Road House, Ghost, City of Joy, North and South, Love and War, Point Break, Red Dawn*. I have seen all of Patrick's movies, and many multiple times, but not as many times as *Dirty Dancing.*

I have always liked movies and can't name all the ones that I have seen. I worked in a movie theater and Blockbuster too. So that's way too many. My favorite animated is *Lion King.*

Have you ever met Patrick or anyone else from the cast?

Unfortunately, no. When I was younger, it was my fondest wish to meet Patrick! Of course, I'd still like to meet the man who helped me through some tough stuff, but realistically I know that won't happen.

Will you continue to watch *Dirty Dancing*?

I haven't stopped yet and I don't think I ever will! When it comes on TV, I still get caught in the story and can't change the channel. As an adult, I can now appreciate the fact that it was a well written film. Everyone my age loves DD and Patrick Swayze.

What do you think about *Dirty Dancing*, the movie being made into the stage production, and do you plan on seeing it?

Is Patrick in it? LOL. I think it's great but I don't expect it to be as good as the original '87 version. Mostly because I think Patrick helps make the story come alive in a way no other actor can or could.

Do you think a sequel could be made?

Technically, there is a *Dirty Dancing* sequel. It is *Dirty Dancing: Havana Nights*. Patrick is a dance instructor in the movie . . . I would truly love to see Patrick do an ACTUAL sequel because in my heart *Havana Nights* isn't a sequel. LOL.

Anything else you want to say about *Dirty Dancing*?

Just that it is a great movie! Patrick did an awesome job in the role as "Johnny Castle," as did Jennifer Grey as "Baby."

On a more serious note, I am saddened to hear about Patrick having pancreatic cancer. I pray that he will be able to make it through this tough time in his life. I'm sending him all my strength that I can!!!!!!

Additional Demographic Information

Marital Status: Happily married to the man of my dreams

Education: Some college

Profession: Homemaker (son—age 13)

Official Patrick Swayze International Fan Club member: Joined in 2007

ROY HELTON

Age 35. Lives in Ferndale, Michigan.

September 2008 (written interview).

*Roy's mother—Barbara Phipps (age 62) also did an interview.

Has seen *Dirty Dancing* 16–50 times.

What year did you first see *Dirty Dancing*? And how old were you?

1988. Sixteen.

Why do you like *Dirty Dancing* so much?

It made me feel good and that dreams can come true.

How has *Dirty Dancing* impacted you personally?
On the questionnaire, you checked off, "has given hope that love exists" and "has given hope that people will do the right thing." Could you say anything more specific about this?

By believing that hope can bring positive things in your life.

People in general are good and want to help others.

In addition to *Dirty Dancing*, how many movies have you seen multiple times? Is Patrick in them?

Bridget Jones, Muriel's Wedding, Steel Magnolias, Star Wars.

Have you ever met Patrick or anyone else from the cast? If so, what was it like?

Met Patrick one time at dinner [following a benefit gala that Patrick hosted in Detroit for the dance company—Complexions].

Will you continue to watch *Dirty Dancing*?

Yes.

What do you think about *Dirty Dancing*, the movie being made into the stage production? Do you plan to see the stage production?

I think it will be a huge success. Yes.

Do you think a good sequel can be made?

I think the sequel came out too late and did not capture the same energy and passion that *Dirty Dancing* had.

Anything else you want to say about *Dirty Dancing*?

Dirty Dancing is a movie that has impacted many generations in my family's life. It is one of the few movies we all can identify with and enjoy sharing.

Additional Demographic Information

Marital status: Single

Education: MA in Psychology

Occupation/Profession: Mental Health

Official Patrick Swayze International Fan Club member: No

BECKY WILLIAMS

Age 36. Lives in Macomb, Michigan.

May 28, 2008 (in-person interview).

Has seen *Dirty Dancing* countless times.

What year did you first see *Dirty Dancing*?

I saw it in '87 . . . when it came out . . .

How old were you?

I was fifteen when I first saw *Dirty Dancing* . . .

You said you were a fan of Patrick before?

I was a fan of Patrick before the movie came out . . . Yes, I became a fan of Patrick when I saw *North and South* . . . He captured me then, and he's had me captured ever since . . . I have seen *North and South* probably almost as many times as I've seen *Dirty Dancing*.

How many times have you seen *Dirty Dancing*?

Oh, countless. I tried to come up with a number and I don't even think I can hazard a correct guess . . .

Have you seen *North and South* almost as many times?

Dirty Dancing is so much easier because it's such a shorter timeframe, but certain episodes certain themes from *North and South* . . . again, just countless times. I absolutely love the story, and you know he makes it that much better—so both of them.

When did you first see *North and South*?

North and South sometime around '84 . . . or right before then.

And you said you would love to meet Patrick and that you are not usually a celebrity fan.

I am not a star struck individual. He is the one and only that I have, you know, a real yearning to meet and talk with.

Do you think you will meet him?

I hope so. It has become that much more important to me since he's been ill, and I don't know whether that is right or wrong, but I would love to meet him . . . if nothing else to let him know the real impact that he's had on me . . .

What do you think that impact is?

I think earlier you said something about the book being sort of like a dream or call it a passion . . . He's made that very real for me through his work . . .

I've just developed a real healthy, not an obsession affection . . . a healthy affection . . . I think sometimes so many people can get really obsessed with a famous celebrity or individual, and I don't want that to be confused with . . . I have no unhealthy notion of anything, but you know a good conversation and just really sharing with him the impact that he's had on my life.

What impact is that?

I think he has helped to develop that dream . . . you know two of his stories—both *North and South* and *Dirty Dancing*—have been escapes for me . . . they've been havens . . . they've been places to go . . . It's kind of like a favorite food, or a blanket or a cup of hot chocolate—just some place comfortable to go . . . a get-away . . . And he's helped create those places through his art. Just to watch him dance.

You know on the questionnaire on #3, you had checked off, "has provided relief in a difficult time," "has given hope that love exists," "has been an emotional catharsis," "has given hope that people will do the right thing." We already covered some of that. Is there anything else that you want to say about #3?

I think one of the things *Dirty Dancing* does for me is that sometimes people think that when you have a love for something, it needs to end happy. And I think *Dirty Dancing* was a story that love wasn't necessarily going to work out—it wasn't necessarily going to continue or necessarily go anywhere, but they could live in that moment. I like that thought that you can just live in the moment without having to worry about what may come after . . . that is one of the things that I love about it. You just knew that even though it sort of ended happy . . . I don't have any misconceptions that they were going to be together forever . . . but that they could just have their time . . .

You were just speaking about how *Dirty Dancing* allowed that something can be for the moment, that it's sort of not just happiness forever.

And I think the other thing that it does for me is that I think it shows that sometimes even though you do the right thing, it doesn't mean that someone's not going to get hurt. When you do the right thing, there are people that are going to get hurt.

Are you talking about when Baby said Johnny didn't steal the wallet?

Oh gosh, there are so many . . . there's that . . . there's I think one of my favorite examples of that in the movie—I think probably frustrates most people, but I understand why he did it. I mean Johnny had several opportunities to tell her father the truth about the baby and chose not to . . .

So when you do the right thing, sometimes people get hurt?

There are examples of that all over the movie.

Are you saying in other words, that the movie in some regards is realistic?

Yes, in that regard, definitely.

I also think there are some people that aren't used to people doing the right thing for them.

One of my favorite lines of the movie is: "Nobody has ever done anything like that for me." I think that is a very important part of the movie. It is one of the most realistic parts of the movie. You really believe him when he says that. She (Baby) truly never hesitates to do the right thing in the movie . . . I don't think she ever hesitates any time that she does the right thing. She just does what you should do.

Now, did you hear Patrick talk on the 20th anniversary DVD? He said the movie could never have been made without Jennifer Grey—that no one else could have done the role. No one else could have captured Baby like she did. Do you think that is true?

I do. I think the casting was ideal . . . I can't picture it cast any differently.

I doubt that the movie would be the same if the casting was different because characters were essential to the emotion of the story. I think they got it right . . . I think it was magic. That's what I mean about the stage production . . . I just don't see how it's going to get pulled off. I think the story is only part of why it is such an icon. I think the casting is essential to that. I can't picture anyone else in any of the roles.

I personally have trouble picturing anyone else as Johnny.

Yeah, that definitely wouldn't have been the same.

You spoke about *North and South* and *Dirty Dancing*—seeing them a lot of times. Are there any other movies that you watch a lot of times, whether Patrick is in them or not?

There are. I have seen a lot of his things several times. I've seen every one of his movies at least once or more. I own all of his movies. I do have a couple other—what I refer to as cult classics or movies—that I have watched several times over. I have my favorites. *The Breakfast Club* is one of them . . . I think that was because of the actors I grew up with. But then I just have some favorites too. *The Shawshank Redemption* is a favorite of mine that I have seen several times. My husband and I really like *A League of Their Own*. We are such baseball fans. We think it is a really good story and again I think the casting in that is superb. (Per Becky's notes, she has seen *Ghost*, *The Outsiders*, *Red Dawn*, *Road House* many times.)

Will you continue to watch *Dirty Dancing*?

Of course. I can't wait for my daughter to be old enough to share it with her.

How old is she?

She is eleven . . . I don't think she is quite ready yet . . .

I can watch it over and over, and I never get tired of it. I still have friends that if they're flipping channels and they see it, they'll call me. Not like I don't own eighteen different copies of the DVD.

Is there anything else you want to say about Dirty Dancing?

I find it almost difficult to even put in to words—how it moves me. How I can absolutely become caught up in it—even though I know exactly what's going to be said, exactly what's going to happen. Every time I watch it, it's almost like I'm as captured as I was the first time I saw it. I never get tired of it. I'll still smile, I'll still laugh, I'll still cry . . . And I think that's the sign of a real good story.

What do you think about a *Dirty Dancing* sequel? Can it be done?

No, because again, I don't believe the story goes on from there. I believe they touched each other in that moment. They changed each other both in some ways, but in that era that relationship was not going to last from there.

Do you know about when you joined the fan club?

Only within the last year.

Do you ever watch it with your husband?

I have. He thinks I am a little off. I always tease him that I was in love with Patrick way before he ever came along. He knew where he stood.

He will even laugh and even make fun of me at times because I will get so caught up in it (DD) like I've never seen it before, and he just finds it very humorous.

Patrick and *Dirty Dancing* and *North and South* are just part of who I am. My friends and family know . . . I can't tell you the number of cards, letters, and e-mails I got, when he got sick . . .

I never would have thought that someone that I had never met before would have such an impact on me . . .

I think that there are a lot of people like that (from reading the guestbook).

I understand where they are coming from. He is a special individual. He's got to be to have captured me the way he has. There's something there. I think it goes beyond charisma. There are a lot of people that have charisma that haven't captured me the way he has.

Like I said, what cracks me up . . . so many people . . . that know how enamored I am with him, say, "You know he is married." Yes, I am very much aware, that is not what this has to do with, and partly, that's what impresses me so much about him . . . a thirty-three year Hollywood marriage . . . You just don't do that. You have to be quite a special individual. Don't you? I think . . . He's had the opportunity to seek so many more lucky roles, and he has chosen to do only things that he wanted to do . . . He could have been so much more in the limelight.

We covered a lot of ground. I appreciate it.

I think he's an easy subject to talk about. *Dirty Dancing* is an easy subject to talk about.

For the first time since Patrick got ill, just in the last week I've been able to start watching something with Patrick in it. I watched the commentary on the 20th anniversary. Patrick talked about how he is so amazed by the multi-generation fan base for DD and something like how he realizes fans have put him where he is (which I have heard him say before).

I remember the day that I found out . . . that the news broke that he was ill. I came home and I started rifling through all of the DVDs. My husband finally came up behind me and said, "Can I help you find one?" and I said, "I am looking for the *North and South* commentary. I don't want to see him acting in a role. I want to see him talking." I just had that need to see him—not in character—Patrick . . .

Do you watch the *North and South* commentary?

Yes, it's fantastic if you haven't seen it . . . Unlike some of the other commentaries, it really is Patrick Swayze, James Reid, Leslie Ann Dowe . . . very nuts and bolts . . . And he's Patrick—typical—genuine . . .

Did you see *One Last Dance*?

Oh, yes. I've seen all of his movies. Every one of them. I own them all. When I say I am a fan, I am a fan.

I think that we have really have covered a lot of ground.

I hope I was able to give you something additional—something different.

You have.

Good.

It's really interesting because a lot of people say some of the same things, but then everybody has their own view of it or their own things that strike them about it or resonate with them.

I think the only other thing is when we had talked about living in the moment. My absolute favorite line of the movie, and why I think it's that living in the moment. My absolute favorite part of the movie is when she looks at him and says, " . . . I'm scared of walking out of this room and never feeling the rest of my whole life the way I feel when I'm with you."

I think everyone needs to feel that in their lives, even if it is not the person you spend the rest of your life with . . . just that feeling, at that moment . . .

Additional Demographic Information

Marital Status: Married

Education: BA from Central Michigan University

Profession: Medical Office Manager

KELLY MINER

Age 37. Lives in Southfield, Michigan.

March 11, 2009 (in-person interview).

Can you tell me what year you first saw *Dirty Dancing*?

I actually saw it when it first came out in 1987 and I was actually in high school in the 10th grade. And now, I'm thirty-seven.

So you were about sixteen?

Yes, about sixteen years old.

How did you hear about the movie? Did somebody tell you about it? Did you see it in the paper?

I'm actually a "moviehead." I love movies. I like anything with music, dancing, comedy, love. I come from a family where both of my parents are professional musicians, so I just have it in me.

So both of your parents are musicians. Tell me about that.

My dad is seventy-eight now. My mom is seventy-six now. They originally worked at Detroit Public Schools as teachers and they were the music program. Basically, they had a glee club and they were basically over the music department for a school on the east side of Detroit called Lilly Bridge Elementary. But unfortunately, in the mid '80s as we all know, some inner cities got hit hard, and they took music out of some of the Detroit public schools. So my parents were basically forced to teach 6th and 2nd grade. They are musicians. My dad actually still has a music school in Detroit where he teaches music, voice, and guitar lessons. So he still teaches, but when they were in their careers, unfortunately their music careers were cut short due to the economic times in the Detroit Public School system which unfortunately still exists today—which is kind of ironic.

When you saw it the first time, did you see it by yourself or with somebody?

I know I was with at least three girlfriends.

So how many times do you think you've seen *Dirty Dancing*?

Around ten. I just recently saw it over Christmas time. It was on DEMAND and I watched it.

So why do you like *Dirty Dancing* so much?

Well one, because of Patrick Swayze. I always liked him. He's hot, and just a good guy.

Was that from the very first time you saw him?

Yes. And then, it is not only a love story but it's also a fun story. It's comedy too. And it's also about family and the relationship that she had with her father, and I am really close with my father so I bonded with that story line as well. And kind of about social class too. It didn't matter what social background you came from. Everybody got along.

That's a lot of reasons. How do you think *Dirty Dancing* impacted you personally? Any of the choices from the questionnaire apply to you?

It definitely gave me hope that love still exists. I think that it shows love on many levels. I mean even the love he had for the people he worked with and how they looked out for each other, and then the relationship he had with Jennifer Grey's character. I liked that—the whole looking out for each other, unconditional love. Everybody had each other's back. I really liked that. Also, I think it did give hope that people will do the right thing. Towards the end, the father lightened up because he kind of had pre-judged him (Johnny) for his lifestyle, and then he realized how much his daughter really loved him, and how he was good for his daughter. I think in the end, it showed people are about doing the right thing.

In addition to *Dirty Dancing*, are there other movies that you've seen many, many times? And if so is Patrick in them?

Ghost. I love *Ghost*. I've seen that a lot. *The Outsiders*. I was a big *Outsiders* fan. I've seen that many times.

Are there other movies though, that Patrick is not in, that you've seen a lot of times?

It's an older movie. It's called *Sparkle*—Irene Cara was in it and Philip Michael Thomas. It was about three sisters that were entertainers. It came out in the late '70s. I've seen that movie at least thirty times.

Anything else?

Imitation of Life. There are two versions. The one with Lana Turner—that one I've seen about I would say about twenty times. There are two of them. There is one that came out like in the fifties and then that one I think came out in the seventies but Lana Turner was the actress in the one I like . . . It was about two women, a black women and a white woman, and both had daughters and the black daughter actually looked white, and so she was passing as white. People were finding out she wasn't a white girl . . .

Have you ever met Patrick or anyone else from the *Dirty Dancing* cast?

No, I have not.

Will you continue to watch *Dirty Dancing*?

Yes, it was fun, and if I ever have children—that's it—that's the kind of movie that anybody can relate to that you would show the younger generation. So it's definitely kind of like a *West Side Story* kind of movie where everyone just sees it because it's like nostalgia. I definitely will watch it again. I'll probably end up getting the twenty–year DVD.

What do you think about the movie being made in to a stage production?

Definitely, 'cuz it's basically music so it would fit right into like a play. I think that would go off very well. I would go see it. It definitely has all the elements for Broadway.

What do you think about a movie sequel being made at this point?

If they do it right. And what I mean by do it right is like maybe add new, fresh characters, but yet don't forget the old characters . . . It should stand on its own though 'cuz sometimes when people do sequels, I think they mess up because if someone hasn't seen the first movie, a lot of people can't relate to the second movie . . .

What other things do you want to say about *Dirty Dancing*?

I just think that anybody that's into music and dancing—it's just another genre of dancing that we should take heed to. And just like everybody is trying to own that *Dancing With The Stars*—you know born now. I think DD has its own culture and its own fan base, and I think it will always live because anybody that's into music and dancing will appreciate it. I mean if you are somebody that's into dancing, this is definitely a must see movie if you have not seen it. It's definitely a classic when it comes to that.

It's a movie that you know, so many movies out today are so serious—it lends itself to a sense of fantasy element too, so I think it's just a happy movie. It's a positive movie. Sometimes we see so many dark movies. This is an uplifting movie. And I like the theme song. I really like that.

Do you have a favorite character or scene?
Would you say the finale scene is your favorite?

Actually, the finale scene was good, but I think leading up to it was better—like when they were practicing and she was kind of quirky with it. Jennifer Grey definitely stole the show for me. She was really good. I mean Patrick was good, but just her character being quirky and so naive in a sense. I really liked the character, and she was kind of like timid and she became confident towards the end. She was my favorite character, and he was second to her.

I also liked the scene when the dad finally figured out that Patrick Swayze's character was the one that was helping out with that guy—the guy who was playing on his other daughter. I kind of like how that was revealed—like the bad guy was finally found out.

Additional Demographic Information

Marital Status: Single (never been married)

Education: Eastern Michigan—Bachelor of Science in Telecommunications/ Film
Saginaw Valley State University—Masters in Leadership and Public Administration

Profession: Freelance Television News Reporter—Fox Toledo News
Auto Show Spokesperson (represents Chrysler)

Official Patrick Swayze International Fan Club member: Not yet

Kelly and I then had a discussion about arts in the schools.
I was just commenting about Beyonce and how Beyonce feels about music in the inner city curriculum in schools. She had made a comment, as she's part of the campaign to save the music [SAVE THE MUSIC FOUNDATION], which Gloria Estefan is also part of, and many other well-known artists. But basically, Beyonce said that the reason why she's pulling for schools in the inner city (and just in general all over) to have music in their curriculum—is because if she did not have it in her school at that time, she said she probably wouldn't be the artist that she is today—for the simple fact that she was a shy student, and that she expressed herself through music. So that is why she's very for music in the school system because that's how a lot of the students grow.

I heard Patrick Swayze when he came to the Music Hall (Detroit) twice

(2002 & 2004) and talked about this subject—the importance of the arts for kids. He came with Complexions Contemporary Ballet. They are awesome. They go all over the world giving dance concerts and they do outreach to inner city kids—give dance workshops. Patrick, is on the advisory board of directors (and so is Lisa, his wife), and so he would travel sometimes with the company to have charity benefits. He introduced Complexions Contemporary Ballet—didn't dance. I sat in the front row. It is not the best place to sit to see the dancing, but that is where I wanted to be to see and hear Patrick. In his introductory speeches, he talked about how important the arts are and how the arts distinguish us humans from beasts. Also, he spoke about how important it is to get the kids away from the TV and computer, and get them involved in dance and the arts, before it is too late. He also said that through dance, we can unite the world. After the dance concert (both times), Patrick hosted a gala reception at the Detroit Athletic Club to raise money for Complexions Contemporary Ballet. Patrick gave autographs and pictures.

Note: After Patrick Swayze passed, Mr. Dwight Rhoden, Artistic Director, Co-Founder, and Resident Choreographer at Complexions Contemporary Ballet, created "Mercy"—a two part ballet dedicated to Patrick Swayze. "Mercy" was premiered at the Joyce Theater in New York in 2009.

BARBARA SCHIEBL

Age 41. Lives in Landsburg, Germany.

February 2008 (e-mail interview). August 2008 (e-mail follow-up questions).

Has seen *Dirty Dancing* 101–500 times.

What year did you first see *Dirty Dancing* and how old were you? How did you happen to see *Dirty Dancing*? Did somebody tell you about it? Were you already a fan of Patrick from *North and South*?

I saw it first 1987 and I was twenty-one. I knew Patrick from *North and South* and I loved him . . . I was twenty-one years old and I loved dancing very, very much. I can't remember if anyone told me about this movie, but I remember that I went to the cinema on my own, without any friends, and I loved this film from the first minute. I went to cinema every day (and sometimes twice a day) for about one week, to watch DD.

Why do you like *Dirty Dancing* so much?

It gave and gives me a good attitude towards life. I love the dancing and the music. I love Patrick and it is a big dream of mine to dance with him. I love the story. It's so romantic. It's a real feel-good movie for me.

How has *Dirty Dancing* impacted you personally?

The courage of "Baby" inspired me to find my own courage.

The dancing of Patrick and the others inspired me to find my own way of dancing.

In addition to *Dirty Dancing*, how many movies have you seen multiple times? Is Patrick in them?

I saw *North and South* multiple times and also *One Last Dance* and some other Patrick movies (for instance *Road House*, *Forever Lulu*), but none of them as often as DD.

There are some other movies without Patrick that I also watched multiple times. I think about approximately five.

Have you ever met Patrick or anyone else from the cast?

No, unfortunately not.

I am a great Patrick fan since *North and South* and [the] DVD came out. But after that time, my life had many challenges for me and "to be a fan" has taken a back seat until last year spring. It was March or April when I thought that it would be nice to watch DD again, and I bought the DVD. The movie fascinated me again and I became a member of Patrick's fan club. In this time, I found out that it could get real to meet him one day because on the fan club website were many reports about the possibilities the fans have had in the past to get in touch with him. So it became a very big dream of mine to meet him one day.

Will you continue to watch *Dirty Dancing*?

Yes, at the moment I watch *Dirty Dancing* once a day. It is always a time of a few weeks when I watch *Dirty Dancing* so intensive. Afterwards, I make a pause of a few weeks and then I start again.

What do you think about *Dirty Dancing*, the movie being made into the stage production, and do you plan to see the stage production?

For me, *Dirty Dancing* is connected with Patrick and Jennifer, and I don't plan to see the stage production.

Please say more about your statement on the questionnaire that said: "has given me hope for my life, that I will have the courage to find my way especially in dancing."

I had a sad time with big family differences behind me. Watching *Dirty Dancing* gave me hope because I began to feel like "Baby." I admired the courage "Baby" has in the movie. She stands by her feelings and fights for them against her father and society. I had worked hard for many years to find my way and with watching *Dirty Dancing* again and again (last spring) my change in this part began. I had to become forty-one years old to tell my parents my point of view—not accepting bad compromises. And now I feel comfortable with my decision.

I rediscovered my love for dancing. I loved dancing so much since I was a teenager until I was about twenty-five years old. After this time, I was very interested in martial arts, qigong, and taiji. My love for dancing had taken a back seat. I graduated trainings as a qigong teacher and women's self-defense teacher. I worked freelance in both areas besides my main job in an office. But ten years later, I stopped teaching qigong and women's self-defense because I did not know if it really was the way I want to go. Afterwards, I only practiced taiji for myself. And after some years, DD came again into my life and inspired me to find my own way of dancing. I always wanted to do partner dancing, but most of the time I had no partner. Now I want to find my way of single dancing. I'd like to express my feelings in dancing. I'd like to get in touch with my body in a completely new way. I'd like to become fit and flexible in my movements and to find my own rhythm. And perhaps I'd like to teach my kind of dancing one day.

What do you think of a *Dirty Dancing* movie sequel being made? Do you think it could be successful?

For me, the *Dirty Dancing* movie with Patrick is the only one. I think it was such a piece of luck . . . this story, with this music and these actors.

Additional Demographic Information

Marital status: Single

Education: O-level (in German "Mittlere Reife")

Profession: I'm a banker . . . [and] nine years working in the social area as an administrator, Freelance qigong teacher

Official Patrick Swayze International Fan Club member: Yes, since 2007

FLABIA PENNELLA

AGE 41. Lives La Plata, Argentina.

July 2008 (e-mail interview).

Has seen *Dirty Dancing* countless times.

What year did you first see *Dirty Dancing*? How old were you?
Did someone tell you about the movie or did you just happen to hear about it? Did you initially watch it by yourself or with someone else?

I first saw the movie in 1990. I was twenty-three. I saw the movie by mistake, because I wanted to see a dance movie from Central America called *Baile Caliente* (hot dancing). I was convinced that DD was that movie, but to my surprise, I was so moved by DD that I saw it twice in a day. I was with one of my cousins. Both of us fell in love with Patrick that very moment.

Why do you like *Dirty Dancing* so much?

I loved the film so much for many reasons. The story was true to life. I love the kind of men that have the guts to fight for love. In such a controversial and material world, the role of love is worth being mentioned. Patrick's acting was perfect as well as the rest of the cast, and the music—a great variety of it was really well selected.

How has *Dirty Dancing* impacted you personally?
On the questionnaire #3, you checked off, "has given hope that love exists," and "has given hope that people will do the right thing." Anything more you want to say about the above?

Dirty Dancing has impacted me personally because of the topic itself. The fact that you have to fight for your feelings and beliefs.

In addition to *Dirty Dancing*, how many movies have you seen multiple times? And is Patrick in them?

Since *Dirty Dancing*, I've seen all Patrick's movies, thousands of times. I can recite them all.

Have you ever met Patrick or anyone else in the cast? If so, what was that like?

Unluckily, I have never met him. That was my dream, but it has never come true.

Will you continue to watch *Dirty Dancing*?

I still love watching it. I also bought the CD with the music.

What do you think about the movie being made into a stage production?

I think it would be great.

Do you think a sequel could be made (*Dirty Dancing 2*)?

I think a sequel could have been made with Patrick. I don't know if there's anyone who can replace him or take his role. If so, he must be and do an excellent work to succeed.

Is *Dirty Dancing* very popular in Argentina?

From my view point, *Dirty Dancing* became much more popular in my country in the mid-90s. I believe *Ghost* was much more popular, but perhaps because of the topic it deals with. Since Patrick got ill, there have been specials on TV Sunday afternoons where you can enjoy all his movies, including DD.

Anything else you want to say about *Dirty Dancing*?

It's a great movie. All the people involved in it must feel pride and inner emotions. Twenty years is a long period of time, and if the movie is still on, it must have been a really good one.

Additional Demographic Information

Marital status: Divorced

Education: Complete education

Occupation: English teacher in La Plata, Argentina

Official Patrick Swayze International Fan Club member: No

KARI THOMPSON

AGE 51. Lives in Idaho.

May 2009 (e-mail interview).

Has seen Dirty Dancing 16–50 times.

What year did you first see *Dirty Dancing*? How old were you? Did someone tell you about the movie or you just happened to hear about it? Did you initially watch it by yourself or with someone else?

Honestly, I don't remember the year. We went to the theater to see it and I was amazed at the incredible talent of Patrick Swayze. I wanted to be his partner! He was sexy but kind, in an innocent way. I went home and danced for hours. I bought the soundtrack when it came out and have worn out three! My entire family went to see the movie. Even my father loved it.

Why do you like *Dirty Dancing* so much?

It teaches that we need to not judge someone based on their looks or attitude. "Bad boys" aren't really bad. It's a mask they wear. A sort of protection, if you will. If you get beyond the facade, you will find sincerity, compassion and also many hard knocks. People can rise above their circumstances and they can change their stars.

The love and gentleness that is shown to Baby is endearing.

How has *Dirty Dancing* impacted you personally?

Include any of these, if applicable:
"has provided relief in a difficult time" (not applicable)
"has given hope that love exists" *(applicable)*
"has been an emotional catharsis" (not applicable)
"has given hope that people will do the right thing" *(applicable)*

Please tell me what about your involvement with dance.

Please elaborate on how Patrick Swayze inspired you.

Dirty Dancing inspired me to take lessons. I wanted to be more free in movement and not so blocked in certain steps. *Dirty Dancing* and Patrick Swayze inspired me to be free in my dancing and to let go of fears. Through Patrick, I have been more confident in myself and have enjoyed the beauty of dance in all forms.

My husband and I have taken dance lessons and we are into ballroom, salsa, and of course, dirty dancing. Most of the students are 30+ single moms.

I had taken ballroom in high school and did well, especially with swing. Michael (my husband) and I chose to take lessons together after *Dirty Dancing*. Michael had been dancing for many years when I met him. We met on a blind date. He was in an original dinner theater production, *Not the Count of Monte Cristo* in Arizona. He danced and sang. I had just come from Hawaii and had been doing disco there. We blended our dancing together and took lessons.

Please tell me how *Dirty Dancing*/Patrick Swayze inspired an at-risk teen to dance.

My husband and I were guardians of a fourteen year old girl who came to us from an unstable and emotionally abusive home. The first night here she wanted to watch *Dirty Dancing*. We put it on and she sat transfixed. After the movie, we took the soundtrack and played it. She began dancing like Baby. It was amazing to see her so comfortable and feeling sure of herself.

During her stay with us we would let her "dirty dance." She watched the movie at least fifteen times while here and got better and better with her dancing. She is now in dance class that we are paying for and she has gone from D's and F's to B's. She feels better about herself and seems to be moving in a good direction in her life. Perhaps some day she will use her dancing talents to find her dream, and perhaps she will be able to inspire others like the movie inspired her. She is still watching *Dirty Dancing* every week.

She looks at boys and compares them to Patrick Swayze. He is the "model of a real man" in her opinion. I have to agree. They broke the mold when he was made.

In addition to *Dirty Dancing*, are there movies that you have you seen multiple times? If so, is Patrick in them? And how many have you seen multiple times?

Road House, seen it at least fifteen times.
Ghost, I have seen at least one hundred times!
We have also watched *Ever After* over fifty times!
Willow at least twenty.
Chicago, dozens of times.

Have you ever met Patrick Swayze or anyone from the cast? If so, what was it like?

No, we have not had the honor of meeting him or anyone from the cast.

In 1993, my husband took master classes from Patsy Swayze (Patrick's mom) at her dance studio. She was fantastic. He said it was awe-inspiring to dance where someone like Patrick Swayze had learned. The energy there was awesome. He also attended another master class at the studio hosted by ABT.

Will you continue to watch *Dirty Dancing*?

Yes, at least three to four times a year, if not more.

What do you think about *Dirty Dancing*, the movie being made into the stage production, and do you plan to see the stage production?

It will be hard for anyone to be like Patrick. However, Adam Lambert would be fantastic in the role.

Yes, we would go see it, definitely.

Do you think a movie sequel could be made?

NO. Don't mess with perfection.

Is there anything else you want to say about *Dirty Dancing*?

The movie gives a person the feeling that you can be anything you want to be. You don't have to be locked into a stereotype. There is so much out there to enjoy and experience if we allow ourselves the opportunity to be free. Everyone should be able to "dance" and be "like the wind."

Additional Demographic Information

Marital status: Married

Education: Grad School

Occupation/Profession: Writer and animal rescuer

Official Patrick Swayze International Fan Club member: Since 1995

CRYSTAL L. BERGER

Age 53.

Lives in Birch Bay, Washington.

January 2008 (e-mail and telephone interviews).

July 2008 (e-mail interview).

Has seen *Dirty Dancing* 51–100 times.

When did you first see *Dirty Dancing*?

Summer of 1989.

So *Dirty Dancing* wasn't the first movie you saw Patrick in?

Yes, it was.

Why do you like *Dirty Dancing* so much?

I fell in love with Patrick's voice. I had heard the song "She's Like The Wind" in London playing everywhere. My neighbor told me about the movie. I rented DD and fell in love with the whole movie.

I remember the era. I was too young to be part of it so *Dirty Dancing* let me live vicariously. It is an age before our world view became more cynical. It resonates with me.

Dirty Dancing lets me get away from life's problems and takes me to a place that I feel safe. I fell in love with the entire cast. Baby, Johnny, the dancers—the casting was perfect.

It has been a lovely friend through many years.

How has *Dirty Dancing* impacted you personally?

It helped me through my cancer treatment. I mentioned that I loved *Dirty Dancing* and the nurses related to it. They knew what I was talking about without any explanation. (Interestingly, the nurses were twenty years younger than me.) They played the music for me. They talked about how wonderful Patrick was in this movie. We could go somewhere else besides the radiation room during my treatments. It was something positive in a difficult situation.

It kept me from moping and dwelling on things.

In addition to *Dirty Dancing*, how many movies have you seen multiple times? And is Patrick in them?

I haven't watched any other movie multiple times. DD is like a nice cup of tea and a good book on a rainy day.

Have you ever met Patrick or anyone else from the cast?

I met Patrick in Houston (2003) when *One Last Dance* was premiered. He was very gracious.

In Houston, did you get a chance to tell Patrick about *Dirty Dancing* helping you with your cancer treatment?

No, cancer was after Houston (January 13, 2004–2005).

I will always be grateful to Patrick Swayze and DD for helping me through this cancer. It is odd, I found the lump in my breast in LA the night two friends and I were going to see Patrick in *Chicago*. So I guess the Swayze will always be part of me so to speak.

Will you continue to watch *Dirty Dancing*?

Yes. It is a lovely movie and I never tire of watching it. I don't watch too often, but at least once a year I will pull it out and sit down and enjoy it all over again.

Does your husband watch *Dirty Dancing* with you?

My husband will watch it about every three years. LOL!

He loves *Ghost*. It's one of his favorite movies. He will sit down anytime to watch *Ghost* with me.

What do you think about *Dirty Dancing*, the movie being made into *Dirty Dancing*, the stage musical? Do you plan on seeing the *Dirty Dancing* stage musical?

To me, *Dirty Dancing* is Patrick Swayze, Jennifer Grey, and the rest of the wonderful cast. They brought a special magic to the roles that can't be duplicated. It was a special moment caught on film. There will only be one Rhett Butler and only one Johnny Castle. I don't plan on seeing the stage production. I watch the movie when I need some charmed time, a little bit of sweetness.

What do you think about a *Dirty Dancing* movie sequel?

I don't think I would like to see a sequel—simply because *Dirty Dancing* caught a magic moment that can't be repeated. I wish they could but I don't think so. I guess I am the only one that wants them to just leave *Dirty Dancing* be the way it is. You can't catch lightning in a bottle more than once. But I hope he proves me wrong!!!!

What else do you want to say about *Dirty Dancing*?

A friend sent me a 10x12 color shot of Patrick's derriere from the movie *Road House*. I took a copy in to show the nurses what I was thinking of during radiation treatment. They were the nicest bunch of women. I laughed to myself when one nurse kept the copy of his Beautifulness, LOL! I called the radiation machine "Hal" after the movie *2001* because it reminds me of Hal. So I was lying with my eyes closed and that machine swung over my face. I kept my eyes closed and said, "Good morning Hal" and was radiated. When that section was finished, I opened my eyes and about an inch from my eyes was that picture of Patrick's derriere taped over Hal's eye! I laughed so hard I almost fell off the gurney . . . Here is the follow-up story. I went in for a check-up one day and one of the nurses pulled me over to the nurses' station and said, "Look what we did with Patrick. We fought so bad over who could take him home that we decided on this." There was a 10x12 color photo of a beautiful horse hanging right over the nurses' station on a bulletin board. She walked over and lifted up the horse photo and there was

Patrick in all his glory. They tacked up the two corners so they could walk by and take a peek! These women hid him right out in public! I thought it was wonderful. Then the nurse walked in and said how it cheered her up every day. They were so funny and proud that they figured out such a wonderful solution!

I also have a *Dirty Dancing* 3D stand-up in my room. It makes me smile every time I go in there.

Dirty Dancing is just a gem. They managed to capture a really wonderful moment there . . . that's really nice.

I just love how a woman twenty or eighty is in the same space about *Dirty Dancing*. It gets everybody going.

They got the clothing right. When Baby walks down the bridge the first time, she had a peasant blouse on. She reminded me of wanting a peasant blouse.

Dirty Dancing is part of the fabric now in the United States and everywhere. It pops up everywhere.

Dirty Dancing and Patrick Swayze bring happiness. They are a happy jinx.

Additional Demographic Information

Marital status: Married thirty years

Education: College

Profession: Administrative assistant

Official Patrick Swayze International Fan Club member: Yes, since 2001

DEBBIE WALLERSTEIN

Age 54. Lives in Deerfield Beach, Florida.

March 2008 & July 2008 (e-mail interviews).

Has seen *Dirty Dancing* 101–500 times.

What year did you first see *Dirty Dancing*? And how old were you?

I first saw *Dirty Dancing* on August 26, 1987. I was thirty-four years old.

Why do you like *Dirty Dancing* so much?

I went to see it because I loved Patrick Swayze, but I fell in love with it because it made me feel happy, peaceful, and care-free.

How has *Dirty Dancing* impacted you personally? I know that you have already made some wonderful comments on this questionnaire. I was wondering if there was anything else that you wanted to add or reiterate.

Questionnaire comments: I was already a Swayze fan when the movie came out, so that's why I went to see it. But WOW! I was very ill at the time and alone. My family was thousands of miles away. I was too sick to work and very depressed. I went to the movies every day—sometimes twice a day. After the first week, I think I knew every word. The movie has sustained me and made me smile in the darkest of times for many years.

Interview: As I said, because of the way *Dirty Dancing* made me feel, it helped me through a very terrible personal health ordeal, during which I almost died—my entire way of living changed (I was forced to leave my home and move in with my parents) and during which I was fired from my job because of my illness. It was a dark, lonely, desperate, and terrifying time. But when I was in that theater, I could smile and feel good, safe, and healthy for a few hours. The movie really became a kind of lifeline for me.

In addition to *Dirty Dancing*, how many movies have you seen multiple times?

At least 100, but none as often as *Dirty Dancing*. (*Butch Cassidy*, *The Sting*, all three *Lord of the Rings*, *High Noon*, *Slap Shot*, *The Philadelphia Story*, *Goldfinger*, *Hard Days Night*, *The African Queen*)—it's a long list, and it's all over the map. There's no type.

If so, is Patrick in them?

Only *Point Break* and *Road House* because they are on TV so much.

Have you ever met Patrick or anyone else from the cast?

No.

Will you continue to watch *Dirty Dancing*?

Yes.

What do you think about *Dirty Dancing*, the movie being made into a stage production, and do you plan to see the stage production?

I can't see the reason to do it, and I won't see it. Why spoil perfection?

When did you first become a Swayze fan? Was it from *North and South*?

Yes, I had read the entire *North and South* series. Orry was my favorite character and I became a Swayze fan immediately. Even before *Dirty Dancing*, I had a friend who made me illegal copies of every Swayze video available.

What do you think of a *Dirty Dancing* movie sequel being done?

No! No! Please, no! Why do the powers that be in Hollywood think everything needs a sequel????? I pray they leave a good thing alone, because no sequel made twenty years later could be relevant, interesting, true to the original, not vomit-inducing! The time for a sequel, if there ever was a time, was nineteen years ago, but I don't even think there should have been one then either.

I don't even like the idea that there is a Broadway musical out there! The beauty of DD was its originality. Today's writers and producers just don't seem to have original thoughts. What a pity for all of us.

Anything else that you want to say about *Dirty Dancing*?

I wish they had made a bigger deal about the anniversary!

Additional Demographic Information

Marital status: Single

Education: JD

Profession: Disabled lawyer

Official Patrick Swayze International Fan Club member: I was a member of Swayze's Fan Club beginning in 1988, but I let the membership lapse. Is there a *Dirty Dancing* Fan Club?

CHERYL DUBUQUE

Age 55. Lives in Burbank, California area.

January 2008 & July 2008 (e-mail interviews).

Has seen *Dirty Dancing* 16–50 times.

What year did you first see *Dirty Dancing*?

From the first day it was released in the theatres.

Why do you like *Dirty Dancing* so much?

Patrick Swayze—the dancing—the fact that it was a period piece. Great cast overall. And the story elements. Growing up in upstate New York, and having a cousin that would be around the same age and her going through many of the same things as the characters kind of took me "home again." Plus, I was working with Patrick on his live dance show during that same time period of time—and just seeing what dancers go through first hand compared to what the end result is on screen was fascinating. I think more work, dedication, and passion go into something like this than one can imagine.

And of course, the music. We got to hear Patrick sing "She's Like The Wind." The songs are fun and are reminiscent of my childhood . . . not to mention I love "Hungry Eyes." I could listen to "She's Like The Wind" and "Hungry Eyes" probably a dozen times in a row and not get tired of them.

How has *Dirty Dancing* impacted you personally?

Really in the ways mentioned above. It reminded me of things from my past. It took me back to a time and place where things were simpler. Yet, at the same time—some things never change—social status, one finding their place in this life . . . One is always searching for their place in life. Everyone in life is searching for love, acceptance, financial security . . . We all need to know we have a place and purpose in this life. It's like some things change so much as the years go by, and yet, at the same time, it seems like we are still in the same place we were years ago.

In addition to *Dirty Dancing*, how many movies have you seen multiple times? And is Patrick in them?

Well, for one, *Grandview USA* because I was working with them in reference to running contests for fans, etc. Same with *Red Dawn* since they came out around the same time. I was doing fan mail/fan club stuff for Tommy Howell at the time. I dealt a lot with Tommy's grandfather and with his CPA's office (Kate). Since it was long ago, I don't remember all the circumstances surrounding it—but they decided to run contests where selected fans could get a tour of Warner Brothers lot and could go to the screening and get to meet Patrick and/or Tommy. I can't remember if it was the actors' idea, Warner Brothers or whose . . . but it was great because it gave some kids a chance to meet with the actors and tour a studio lot.

On a side note—the one nice thing I remember is that on a few occasions Rob Lowe came because Patrick or Tommy was away working on something else, and Rob sort of stepped in. I met him there and at the *Without A Word* show and remember thinking what a great guy he seemed to me. He always seemed very polite and very down-to-earth.

Also—from (at the time) knowing the actors personally—it's interesting to see movies several times to look at different elements. For example— the first time around, you can be so focused on Patrick or Tommy's acting that you lose the story line or some of the other people in the story. So— you go the next time to pick up the things you missed the first time.

As someone who also writes—I went to *Red Dawn* probably twenty times when it came out—not only because of Patrick and Tommy—but I love John Milius and he has a habit of putting subtle things into a story— things you really have to look for—like the truck that the kids escape in has a bumper sticker that says "Native" on it—and here they are being invaded by Cuba and the Russians. Milius was/is brilliant with subtle things like that.

Plus, with these two movies—I saw them numerous times when I went to the screenings/contests since I had to attend with the winners. And I dragged a lot of my friends to the theatre to get them to support them. Some were reluctant to go—but afterwards seemed to enjoy the movies.

Another one of Patrick's films that I am drawn into is *Tiger Warsaw*—there is a quality to that and his performance that makes me want to watch it more than once . . .

I watch lots of movies again and again—but usually from the writer's point of view—or because I work with actors (have worked a lot in casting)—so was always looking for new talent and or someone appropriate for a film I may be involved with.

Have watched *The Outsiders* and *One Last Dance* quite a few times too.

And *Loving Lula* (*Along For The Ride*)—I saw before it was even released the first time. It was a screening to give your opinion of what worked, what needed to be fixed, etc. It was fun because it was the first time I had seen Patrick on the big screen in quite awhile. And of course, his character is a writer in the film. It's also great seeing him hit that emotional level that men don't always get to do on screen. Like the first time he says his deceased son's name—in the scene with the two women. When he says "Andrew" and his eyes well up with tears—it makes my eyes well up. I also enjoy the scene at the "adopted" family's house when he stands up for Lulu and what she goes through to get there—to meet the son she had to give up. It's really a great film—and one that probably few people have seen. It has many different elements and emotional levels to it. It had to be fun to play as an actor.

And probably anything that has the word "western" attached to it . . . but that's been mostly TV shows. I love that so many of them are now out on DVD—old and new. I grew up on westerns and love anything "cowboy."

Have you ever met Patrick or anyone else from the cast?

Yes, I worked with Patrick (Lisa and Nicholas Dunn) on the stage version of *One Last Dance* when it was still in the working stages and known as *Without A Word*—it was a black box show, with only the three of them revealing their inner most thoughts on dancing, persevering, and life things in general. I worked with Lynn Griffith who did publicity and helped out in several other capacities. Don (Patrick's brother) was the stage manager. I don't remember meeting other people from the *Dirty Dancing* cast—but have met most of *The Outsiders* and some others (from working in this business for thirty-five years).

I also have a strong connection with Jonathan Jackson (from *Dirty Dancing: Havana Nights*)—his brother, Richard Lee, is someone who has been involved with my production company. Richard Lee and Jon are actually going to re-write one of my western scripts.

Some people in Hollywood laugh—you know the "degrees of separation from Kevin Bacon"—it's kind of like "who can we link with someone Cheryl knows or has worked with"—not so much the new people like the Lindsay Lohans or Britneys, etc . . . but I worked with most of the actors in the '70s, '80s, early '90s at one time or another . . .

Will you continue to watch *Dirty Dancing*?

Oh, yeah. It's funny because sometimes when flipping channels and it's on—I get drawn into it. I may even have to be some place and I'll think to myself, "You really need to get ready to go. You saw this recently. And you have it on DVD—so you really don't need to watch this on TV right now . . ." But I still get drawn in. I find it hard to turn off.

What do you think about *Dirty Dancing*, the movie being made into a stage production, and do you plan to see the stage production?

I think it would be cool. If it came to Los Angeles, I would go. Right now I have too tight of a schedule to travel all over to see it—but Los Angeles, or maybe some place close enough like Vegas—I'd go see it several times.

What do you think about a *Dirty Dancing* movie sequel?

They did have *Dirty Dancing: Havana Nights*—with Jonathan Jackson (his brother, Richard Lee is one of my actors for my films . . .) and they did have the series with Patrick Cassidy (another connection to me—I used to know David and be on the PF set).

Bonanza has kind of presented some of the same questions—they tried the prequel with *The Ponderosa* and most of the die hard *Bonanza* fans were up in arms . . . They did the sequels . . . and the reviews from fans have been very mixed . . .

So there is good and bad to both sides of prequels and sequels.

I mean, if Patrick could come back as Johnny Castle—maybe he owns his own sort of resort club or something—that could be fun. You know—he pulled himself up from feeling like nobody to being somebody . . .

Do you think that there are similarities between Patrick and the character of Johnny Castle that made the role such a good fit for Patrick?

Well, of course, the dancing. And some of the things they probably went through. Not going through exactly the same things—but I am sure as an actor there were things Patrick could draw on.

In real life—being a male dancer (especially one who was into ballet) was one of the things Patrick always said he had to battle—getting into fights or arguments to prove his "masculinity." I'm sure you've heard it in interviews before or read about it. And you have to remember in the '60s and '70s it was a little different than it is today—especially for someone growing up in Texas.

With Johnny Castle, he had to prove to himself he was "worthy." In life, people always have things they have to deal with to prove something (more to themselves than to the world around them). And of course, everyone is looking for acceptance and a place they feel they belong in this world.

Each had their struggles. Even though some of the struggles Patrick has faced may be different from the ones Johnny has faced—the outcome is more or less the same.

Patrick has a knee injury—something he has had forever—and I remember in the '80s during *Without A Word* how he would kind of limp around and be in pain—and then go out on stage and perform as though nothing were wrong. I always wondered where he got the strength to do it. But, it's that passion—you know that driving force that we all have deep inside us. It was as though they were two different people—the one backstage and the one on stage. But that's what dedication and hard work and passion and belief in something are about.

Even though with "Johnny Castle"—it wasn't a knee injury—but he still had obstacles to overcome—like when he said, "One month I am eating ju-ju-bes to stay alive—and now women are stuffing $$$"—it's like his need to survive (food wise, life wise) is sort of like the knee injury vs. the person who has to go on stage and perform. Do you let it knock you down so much that you're becoming non-functioning or do you overcome it? Whether it's for survival or from passion for your art—you have to learn to triumph over it. If you don't, your insides feel like they could die.

Both Patrick and Johnny are "over-comers" and are both people who stand up for something they believe in. And they both prevailed.

As much as it may be overused but "Nobody puts Baby in the corner" wasn't a line by accident. That was Johnny's turning point—one who made him realize that some things in life are worth fighting for and that regardless of his social standing, he was worthy.

In many ways, because of the obstacles Patrick faced in his life, and Johnny faced in his—it helped them both come into their own. They each found that acceptance thing we all look for.

Did you notice any changes in Patrick after the success of *Dirty Dancing*?

He's recognized and accepted more by Hollywood or entertainment standards. But as a person, he seems to be still the same down-to-earth, passionate, caring person he always was. Success hasn't changed him. The only changes I see are the ones that come with age and learning . . . and that has more to do with wisdom and life's experiences that help us overcome our demons. But, you could be a school teacher, a lawyer, a waitress, or a housewife and still have things that are only learned with age and experience. I don't think success has spoiled him any.

Which happened first—*Dirty Dancing* or *Without A Word*? And do you think either project influenced the other?

To be honest, I don't know. Both, I'm sure were works in progress. *Dirty Dancing* was released in 1987—but I don't know how long it took them to actually film it, plan it, etc. Funding takes time—and that is something Patrick wouldn't have been involved in. Many times by the time a movie comes out—two years can go by—even with studio films. Since Patrick didn't write *Dirty Dancing*, but he did write *Without A Word*, I would say that both his performances were probably influenced by his years of dance experience, but I don't think one project necessarily influenced the other.

I'm sure *Without A Word* was a lifetime of writing—even if not literally on paper. It is a very personal piece. *Without A Word* did though, as you know, influence *One Last Dance*. Much of it was the same—only it's like they took the situations and they expanded them. But in *Without A Word* and *One Last Dance* they faced many of the same things—the aging process (the effect dancing has on the body as one grows older), the fear of rejection. In the play, Nicholas Gunn had to face his father— his father didn't want him to dance; his father had pre-conceived ideas about what being a dancer meant. I thought Lisa did a great job with directing *One Last Dance*—she brought different elements to it that they couldn't do on stage.

What was it like working on movies and the stage production with which Patrick was involved?

He's a kind, caring, passionate, gentle soul. Humble is probably another word to describe him. Hollywood is full of egos—but there are a handful that are unique and remain true to their roots and beliefs.

Is there anything else you want to share about your contacts/work with Patrick that would be relevant to this *Dirty Dancing* research project?

I do have a funny story.

I used to do some work for Tommy Howell (fan mail/fan club/ merchandizing type work).

I don't think Patrick knew how big *Dirty Dancing* was going to be. He knew me from working on the play with him (*Without A Word*)—but he also knew I connected up with him through Tommy . . .

One day, I am at my neighbor's apartment—and one of my roommates had a friend over in our backyard visiting with my other roommates . . .

The phone rings—and you can hear the friend yelling all through the courtyard, "Cheryl—get your butt back here!! You won't believe who is on the phone for you."

I go out into the courtyard—and her face is all flushed . . . She goes, "She had me answer the phone because they were doing something else . . ." I was like, "Well who's on the phone for me?"

She starts screaming, "It's Patrick Swayze. He's holding for you—I can't believe I just answered the phone to Patrick Swayze."

I go in the house to take the call and my friend is still freaking out running up and down the courtyard screaming.

Anyway, during the short phone conversation, he (Patrick) said, "I asked Tommy what to do—all these girls are writing me letters now and wanting to buy my stuff . . . I've never been through this before . . . If they want to buy things, Tommy said I should talk to you—you would know about this kind of thing."

He was oblivious to if he should start a fan club, sell his photos . . . He never thought *Dirty Dancing* would take off the way it did . . . I think he was shocked (and humbled) he was getting so much attention."

I think that was my one and only phone call from him—but my friend talked about it for a month—she was still in shock.

If I think on it hard enough, even though it was—what, twenty-five years ago—I can still hear my friend yelling through the court yard!!!

Additional Demographic Information

Marital status: Single

Education: Post-grad in Psychology

Profession: Film Production, Book Publishing, Various Entertainment Related (was involved in casting—also worked in a division of publicity in the '80s for Norman Lear)

Official Patrick Swayze International Fan Club member: No

CALLIE VAN KLEECK & DAVID VAN KLEECK

Age 57. Age 52.

Glendale, Arizona

*Callie and David have been married for 25 years.

May 2008 (e-mail interviews).

Callie has seen *Dirty Dancing* 16–50 times and David 2–15 times.

What year did you first see *Dirty Dancing*? How old were you?

Callie: 1987. Thirty-seven years old.

David: 1987. Thirty-two years old.

Why do you like *Dirty Dancing* so much?

Callie: There are many reasons I like the movie. Mostly the love story between two opposites, as in *Romeo and Juliet*. Typically, I don't care for cliche plots, but this one was done well, and I identified with it due to my own love story with my husband, David.

David: I identified with Patrick's character because "ALL" my relationships had me cast as the guy from the wrong side of life, including and especially my twenty-five year marriage to Callie! She is proper, strong, ethical and a Texas born self-sufficient woman, a very rare find indeed. Patrick's character behaved much the same way I had all my life before God put Callie in my life, and she has saved me from myself.

Callie & David: We BOTH love good storytelling and happy endings where every major character gets what they deserve in the end.

How has Dirty Dancing impacted you personally?

Callie: What "Baby" did in handling the situations that put her family at risk, fortified my resolve that no matter what, I will ALWAYS do the "right thing," regardless of the consequences.

David: Once again, as is usual in Patrick's "character" performances, I recognized my "hot-headed" personality and my "victim" outlook in life, as in "the misunderstood, unfairly treated underdog." Seeing that in myself, as others said they saw in me, forced me to take it to heart and change. The epiphany that I could REALLY change my outlook, started the ball rolling in a straight line towards "growing up." And I had really motivating reasons to follow through: my wife deserved a mature man at her side, and I wanted to BE that man!

Callie & David: We knew it was going to be one of "Our Movies" from that day on, because we BOTH love GOOD romantic movies for our "Date Nights" at home.

In addition to *Dirty Dancing*, how many movies have you seen multiple times? And is Patrick in them?

Callie: At least a dozen or more!

David: More like fifty, I think.

Callie & David: In some cases, we've seen movies twice a year every year for almost twenty-five years now! In some cases, like *Dirty Dancing*, twice in a week! Patrick is in many of them! *Red Dawn*, *Next of Kin*, *Road House*, *Ghost*, *Point Break*, and *Three Wishes*.

Have you ever met Patrick or anyone else from the cast?

Callie & David: Unfortunately, no.

Will you continue to watch *Dirty Dancing*?

Callie & David: Absolutely!

What do you think about *Dirty Dancing* the movie being made into the stage production?

Callie: If it doesn't lose any of the impact the movie has, it would be great—and, I hope, as successful.

David: The movie is so "branded" with Patrick Swayze and Jennifer Grey as the stars that I believe stage play actors involved would have a tough time re-creating the dynamics of that relationship, which helped drive the plot and give real substance to the movie.

Do you plan to see the stage production?

Callie: Possibly.

David: Probably take any family or friends, who are into the Performing Arts and would appreciate the story and message behind it.

Did both of you discover the movie at the same time—maybe even watching it together for the first time?

Callie: I watched it before David did.
David: Callie told me about it, so we agreed to watch it together.

Callie & David: After we watched it together for the first time, we've watched it together more than a dozen times!

Has this movie impacted your relationship at all?

Callie & David: It has served as the centerpiece of MANY of our "Date Nights" throughout our twenty-five years of marriage.

Is there one of you that is more into the movie than the other?

Callie & David: No, we both really enjoy watching the movie, and we usually watch it together.

Do you both enjoy the same things about the movie, or are there differences in what makes the movie enjoyable for you—i.e. especially the male point of view versus the female point of view?

Callie: I enjoy the music, dancing, romance and how well the actors brought the movie to life. From a female "perspective," I feel most young girls dream of finding the kind of man Patrick portrayed, and experiencing that kind of love where you know your man believes in you.

David: I enjoy how much "Baby" (aka Frances) reminds me of Callie. She is quite independent, has an incredibly gentle nature and sincere concern for the well-being of others. From a "male point of view," I think the movie is true to reality and portrays the male ego and a man's need to "prove himself," and improve himself.

Anything else that you would like to say about *Dirty Dancing*?

Callie & David: We were surprised to discover that *Dirty Dancing* is based on the real life experience of the writer. It is among Patrick Swayze's better performances. Both Patrick and Jennifer made their characters believable. Their characters' innocence and idealistic outlook on life was genuine in them both. That drew us into their plight more intensely. We actually felt their pain as they realized life as it truly is, and gained strength from the ordeal. It reminded us both of our own awakening to reality.

Are you saying that Patrick and Jennifer put their own innocence and idealistic outlook on life into the characters that they played?

David: No, not necessarily. I am saying that they made their characters very real and convincingly portrayed them as being innocent (in Baby's character) or having been innocent (in Johnny's character). I believe this made Baby's "coming of age" and Johnny's "standing his ground" transformations that much more emotionally impacting—BECAUSE they were believably consistent in their character portrayals. After all, who hasn't been innocent or had that innocence tested or even shattered? Truth rings true no matter how it is conveyed: music, poetry, stories, movies, interviews, relationships . . .

Could I go a step further and ask, Do you think that in "real life," Jennifer and Patrick are genuine people, so they were able to use that quality in their portrayal of Baby and Johnny?

David: I have not seen enough of Jennifer Grey's movie characterizations to make a solid judgment call on her real life personality. But I will say that her performance in *Dirty Dancing* seemed to me to be garnered from within herself, as if she really empathized with the woman she was portraying who wrote the film from real life incidents in her own past.

However, in Patrick Swayze's case, seeing as many movies as I have of his, I have noticed a common thread of decency and humanity in him (with the possible exception of *Letters from a Killer*). His characters are likable, real, ethical, compassionate, and convey an integrity that is palpable. The proof of this is in the length of his marriage to one woman and their obvious dedication to each other . . . For Patrick and Lisa's marriage to be as good as it is for as long as they've been married takes a REAL man and a REAL woman who are very real with each other all the time. It's hard enough to make a marriage work as an every day couple. Multiply that by a thousand if you are a "famous" couple.

Additional demographic information

Both Callie and David are college graduates. Callie is the CEO of Reliable Outsourcing, Inc. and David is the CEO of Performance Computer Specialists, Inc. Both joined the Official Patrick Swayze International Fan Club in 2008.

MALLORY LONGWORTH

Age 60. Lives in Ann Arbor, Michigan.

January 3, 2009 (in-person interview).

*I was referred to Mallory by Mr. H.M. "Buzz" Scanland, Jr., General Manager at Mountain Lake Hotel, as Mallory had gone there for _Dirty Dancing_ Weekends twice and had been written up in _Newsweek_.

When did you first see _Dirty Dancing_? Did someone tell you about the movie or did you just happen to hear about it?

I saw the movie trailer, and I was in New York with my aunt and uncle . . . It made me want to see the movie . . . I saw it, and it just struck a chord. It was like—I've lived that—not the dancing part, but I worked in the Catskills, you know when I was in college—the serving part of it.

About when did you work in the Catskills?

Oh, it was my second year of college—so 1969, 1970.

And something just kept drawing me back to the movie. And after I'd seen it, I don't know how many times, maybe fifty to sixty, I wanted the poster from the movie. So I asked the theater manager if I could have it, and she said no, but she gave me the name of the advertising agency that was providing it . . . So I got into contact with a man there . . . He said, "I'm going to send you the poster, and I want you to keep in touch with me." I said, "I can't stop seeing it. I just can't stop . . ." He said, "Keep in touch with me . . ." Then I saw it one hundred times, and he said, "I have a surprise for you—I have contacted _Newsweek_ magazine, and they are going to contact you." And I said OK sure, yeah that's going to happen. My son was nine years old. And we came home from somewhere that night, and the phone rang and this lady identified herself as being from _Newsweek_ magazine. She said, "If it is all right, I will call you the next day for an interview," which she did. Then she said, "I am going to send a photographer to you. I am not sure that there will be a picture in the article but we'll see." So the article came out the following week. (Article is: "Getting Down and Dirty" by Charles Leerhsen with Tessa Namuth, December 21, 1987.) And then the guy, Neal Rubin from the *Detroit Free Press* called me for a phone interview.

And this (*Detroit Free Press* article—"Movie makes her do the mambo-not the munch-o" by Neal Rubin) was in 1987?

1988. By this time I've seen the movie one hundred-fifty times, and I was talking to my ex-husband (my son's father), and I said, "You know what, I didn't start a war or do anything bad, and it's a really stupid reason for being in *Newsweek,* but I'm going to be in *Newsweek* this week." And he said, "For what?" And I said, "For seeing *Dirty Dancing* . . ." He said "OK." I said, "Maybe it is my claim to fame." So from the *Newsweek* article, I got a call from a teen from South Carolina or Virginia . . . Actually, her mother called me and asked me if it would be all right if I spoke to her daughter, and I said sure. So then they told me about the very first *Dirty Dancing* weekend at Mountain Lake.

That's amazing.

So I went there, and I met them.

And Buzz was there also, right?

Yes, and he's been just phenomenal.

That's what everyone says that I talk to.

I actually went twice.

So that was in around '88?

That's twenty years ago, but the area was just so beautiful and everything that was in the movie.

What did you do while you were at Mountain Lake?

We went for the weekend—my best friend and I. You know they had showings of the movie of course and there was a dinner dance. The food was good. They had activities, you know.

I had heard that there was a life-size cardboard Patrick. I hear it is pretty battered (actually not usable anymore) now-a-days from all its use.

Of course, I had my picture taken with the cardboard Patrick.

Is there anything more that you can say about why you think the movie resonated with you so much?

It was the time—the timeframe. It was 1963 . . . which she says in the opening. I also come from a Jewish family, and you know Mountain Lake looked just like the Catskills.

And then it was a pure love story. And I am highly influenced by that.

Now, do you still watch *Dirty Dancing*?

Yes.

Do you think you always will?

Uh-huh. I don't think there will be another movie like that for me . . . Although I love girlie movies like *Nottingham Hill*.

Have you seen any other movies—other than *Dirty Dancing*—many, many times?

No.

So this is really a phenomenon specific to *Dirty Dancing*?

Yes . . . It's funny whenever I'm sick and just not feeling well, I put the movie on, and it calms me enough—I know it sounds strange—so that I can sleep, so that I get better.

No. I don't think it sounds strange. I understand what you are saying.

What do you think about the fact that *Dirty Dancing* is now playing as a stage musical production? And do you plan on seeing it?

It's a stage production? I wasn't aware of it.

Yes, it started out in Australia . . . Played in the UK—sold out before it even started. It's been to Germany, recently in Toronto, and now it's in Chicago—then it's going to Boston, to LA, and they're talking maybe Broadway.

It's in Chicago? I'll have to ask my friend to go.

I don't know how much longer it will be in Chicago. Different people have obviously different views on it. Actually, Buzz told me he saw it and highly recommended it.

If Buzz recommended it, I'd go see it. I am going to call my friend as soon as we are done and see about it.

When Patrick was starring in *Guys and Dolls* (Nathan Detroit) in London, England, *Dirty Dancing* was playing across the street. When he was shooting *The Beast* (A&E) in Chicago, *Dirty Dancing* was also on stage there. He was interviewed by the *Chicago Tribune* on November 18, 2008 ("Swayze feels at home in Chicago," by Robert K. Elder). Mr. Swayze was asked about how it was for him to be in Chicago while the stage version of *Dirty Dancing* was playing. Mr. Swayze said, "It's surreal, but nothing new . . . But the other day, we were filming, and my character Barker is crossing the street when two cabs with ads for 'Dirty Dancing' go by!"[13]

That was very cute.

What do you think of the idea that some people talk about *Dirty Dancing*, the movie having a follow-up, a sequel? And I don't mean *Havana Nights*.

I used to think maybe there was the possibility of a sequel with Patrick and Jennifer—with her going to college and being successful and meeting with him, and having it all come back to the dance . . . but I don't think there will ever be another *Dirty Dancing*.

You don't think they will ever make it, or you think if they made it, the movie could never be a success—or both?

I think their attempt at *Havana Nights* sucked. I guess I don't understand why it was that, instead of following Baby and Johnny. I don't know how that could be *Dirty Dancing*.

Mallory then showed me the original *Newsweek* and *Detroit Free Press* articles that she is in and gave me a CD of them. I quickly scanned through the articles. I noticed that the *Detroit Free Press* article said that Mallory had lost almost 50lbs at that point in time—by going to the movie rather than sitting at home eating . . .

I think you are going to like this one better.

The *Detroit Free Press*?

Yes.

This was Thursday, January 7, 1988. WOW!

It was just as it was going to video tape.

I love this . . . The *Detroit Free Press* article refers to you as "the unofficial mascot of *Dirty Dancing*" . . . I love this: "Lesli Rotenberg of Vestron, producer of the movie and video, calls her telephone the 'Patrick Swayze hotline.'" Then the article describes how you saw the movie several times in one day: " . . . sitting through a morning show, coming back around six and returning again at midnight."[14]

Did you think they did a good job with the *Detroit Free Press* article? Are you happy with it?

Yeah.

Wow, you went from size 44 to size 16.
Oh, my gosh, they called you to discuss a possible meeting between you and Patrick Swayze. Did the meeting ever happen?

Good Morning America called me, and they were trying to get Patrick on their program, and they were going to bring me to New York, but instead he went to the *Today Show*. So it never happened.

Have you ever met him?

No.

Do you want to meet him?

I dream about meeting him, you know, about him seeing me and saying hi . . . you know meeting on the street.

You mean literally . . . you know a lot of people say it is my dream to meet Patrick Swayze . . .

No, no . . . I was actually dreaming. It happened a couple of times.

I read from the *Detroit Free Press* article: "Longworth's father has not quite understood it all. Years ago, he kept her from Elvis Presley movies because 'anybody who could move like that had to be an evil influence on a young girl.'"

Uh-huh.

"'My father thinks I'm crazy . . . My aunt thinks I've lost my mind. They're probably right. But some people play golf, you know?'"[14]

That is such a wonderful article.

Again, I think the movie is a positive statement of possibilities.

Are you in touch at the present time with other *Dirty Dancing* fans?

No.

Anything else you want to say about *Dirty Dancing*?

Even today, twenty years later, it still holds its magical feeling for me.

Does your son watch the movie?

No. My son is the love of my love . . . he's my heart, and he knows it.

So he would be what—around thirty?

Yes.

He understands Mom's thing for *Dirty Dancing*?

Uh-huh.

I think this is just an amazing story. If you hadn't pursued getting that poster, I don't know if any of the rest of that would have happened. That's just so amazing.

That was the first thing I had ever done like that . . . Nothing has gotten to me, the way *Dirty Dancing* had.

Thank you.

I am glad that you gave me this opportunity.

Additional Demographic Information

Marital status: Divorced

Occupation/profession: Accountant, controller for a steel plant in Westland

Official Patrick Swayze International Fan Club member: No. I helped start the first fan club. I got a picture from Patrick with a note from Patrick on the back.

BARBARA PHIPPS

Age 62. Lives in Waterford, Michigan.

May 2008, July 2008, & July 2009 (telephone interviews/follow-up).

Barbara's son—Roy Helton (age 35) also did an interview.

Has seen *Dirty Dancing* 101–500 times.

What year did you first see *Dirty Dancing*, and how old were you?

1987. I was about forty-one years old.

Why do you like *Dirty Dancing* so much?

It's fun and sexual . . . My husband and I used to dance. It's romantic to get to do dances together. It's provocative and fun. It was a good, happy time in the '50s—didn't have the stress we have today.

It's very entertaining and it makes me feel good.

**How has *Dirty Dancing* impacted you personally?
On the questionnaire, you wrote, "It shows our kids that good values do count." Could you say anything more specific about this and other ways *Dirty Dancing* has influenced you?**
Baby went to her father to help Penny. Baby stood up for Johnny when it went against her Dad (and that was the worst thing for Baby) because she knew Johnny didn't steal the billfold. Baby stood up for what is right.

Americans are losing their morals. Americans need to get back to morals. We need some heroes and someone to look up to. We need kids to have that drive to work and become winners.

Patrick Swayze was always on TV at my mother's house. My mother is age eighty-two and lives in Kentucky. My mother would put the movie on when I got home from working long hours. It would calm me down. It was very soothing and it allowed me to get a good night's sleep, and start again the next day.

He (Patrick Swayze) has helped me through so many difficult times. The movie reminds me that there are good people. It keeps me having faith. The spirit of the movie gives you faith in mankind

It's the kind of ethics you want to instill in your kids. Johnny worked hard and had good ethics.

It also shows that learning new things can be fun and don't give up on your dreams.

In addition to *Dirty Dancing*, are there movies you have seen multiple times, and if so, is Patrick in them?

I watch *Road House* a lot.

Have you ever met Patrick or anyone else from the cast?

No, I have not but my son, Roy met Patrick at a restaurant in Detroit after the Complexions event. I have a picture on my computer of my son and his friend hugging Patrick.

Will you continue to watch *Dirty Dancing*?

Sure, I always will.

What do you think about *Dirty Dancing*, the movie being made into a stage production, and do you plan to see the stage production?

Yes, I would go see it. I would love it.

What do you think about a movie *Dirty Dancing* sequel?

I don't know if they could do it again—no, it can't be done. It would be hard for people who love the movie to accept a new cast.

Do you watch *Dirty Dancing* with your grandchildren?

Yes, I watch *Dirty Dancing* with my thirteen and ten year old granddaughters for the last three to four years. Rachel, the thirteen year old, loves it.

Anything else that you want to say about *Dirty Dancing*?

The movie brings back the first time you fall for a boy and the things you do. It also brings back memories of a sock hop. It was a big deal to get asked to dance.

The tango and merengue are back in now.

The line "Nobody puts Baby in the corner" is so pervasive and so great.

The cast made that movie—made it into a very endearing movie. I loved the dad. The mother was a perfect mother. The sister was identical to what a sister is.

The story line was beautiful. It was like a Grace Livingston Hill story.

What are Grace Livngston Hill stories like?

She wrote love stories. The good guy wins and overcomes obstacles.

Additional Demographic Information

Marital status: Divorced

Education: College degree & culinary degree

Occupation/Profession: Retired. I've done everything—skilled trades, management/administration, training, and development.

Official Patrick Swayze International Fan Club member: No. Didn't know there is a fan club.

Barbara states she is a three-time cancer survivor.

EVELYN SERIAN

Evelyn passed away on May 27, 2009 while at the Hinds Hospice. I think that she would have wanted this interview to run because I know that she had a huge connection to *Dirty Dancing* and to Mr. Swayze. So I respectfully share the interview.

Evelyn lived in Fresno, California.

The interviews were in February 2008 (telephone interview) & April 2008 (e-mail interview).

Saw *Dirty Dancing* 51–100 times.

What year did you first see *Dirty Dancing*, and how old were you?

2007. Age seventy-three. The first movie I saw with Patrick Swayze was *Ghost* (years ago) and I liked it a lot, but it wasn't until I happened upon *Road House* that everything about him clicked for me. I told a gal at Blockbuster about enjoying him on film, and she suggested I rent *Dirty Dancing*—so I did. I do not know where I was when the film first came out, but have certainly made up for what I missed.

Why do you like *Dirty Dancing* so much?

It has everything in it. I just think Patrick Swayze is absolutely adorable.

He's such a perfectionist. He does everything so perfect.

The music, the dancing . . . everything about it. It's a fun movie.

I just love that scene when Billy opens the door and you see all of the Dirty Dancers.

How has *Dirty Dancing* impacted you personally?

I was at kind of a low period and *Dirty Dancing* upped my spirit and mood.

It sort of invigorated me and lifted my spirit.

In addition to *Dirty Dancing*, are there movies that you have you seen multiple times? And if so, is Patrick in them?

Ghost. North and South. I didn't see *North and South* when it came out twenty years ago, but now I own the movie and book. *City of Joy.* I have seen quite a lot of Patrick Swayze movies.

Have you ever met Patrick Swayze or anyone from the cast?

No.

Will you continue to watch *Dirty Dancing*?

Oh sure. Now and then.

What do you think about *Dirty Dancing*, the movie being made into the stage production, and do you plan on going to see it?

I would like to see the stage production. It is hard to visualize it because so many scenes were outside. Also, some parts were just so beautiful and charming, so I wonder how they could capture that in the stage version.

What do you think about a *Dirty Dancing* movie sequel?

I think there are a lot of people out there who would enjoy the movie even if Patrick is not starring in it. The story line is good, the music and dancing, and with the right actors, I think it would be a success.

After all, there have been so many remakes of wonderful movies from the past and there is always a new crop of viewers that would enjoy it. I, for one, could not see it. However, that doesn't mean squat. With all of the bad movies that are being produced today, it would be refreshing for some to see a new version. The only other thing is that it is still being shown on TV on Demand and some other channels, so I do not think it would be the proper time to make the movie and show it. I don't think it would show the proper respect to the original one.

You wrote that you honestly feel like you know Patrick through the

roles he has chosen. What is your impression of Patrick?

I think he selects roles to extend his own philosophy and values. He plays the characters very convincingly. He is a person with scruples and values. He is sensitive. He plays a person of quality and he is a man of quality. He has a cute personality. He can be a real rascal and cut-up. The wife he has chosen shows his character.

He is just the type of person you would want to have as a friend. He is just a very, very dear man with a good heart. And he is no push-over.

Do you see similarities between Patrick and the character of Johnny?

When he is trying to teach her to dance. He has the same movements in some of his other movies.

Anything else that you want to say?

I just love that scene when Robby says to Johnny, "Do you think you can remember that—what you can and cannot do?" and Johnny says, "Just put the pickle on the plate and leave the hard stuff to me."

Since I have been watching Patrick in movies, I've been broadened. For example, I have read the *City of Joy* book and the *North and South* book (from which I learned about the Civil War).

I feel like seeing Patrick in movies has been a positive force in my life.

Additional Demographic Information

Marital status: Divorced

Education: BA in Liberal Studies

Occupation/Profession: Retired. Retail. Horticulture. Manager for Customer Relations.

Official Patrick Swayze International Fan Club member: Yes, for about one year.

DOREEN HEIGHT

Age 75. Lives in Derby, England.

Has seen *Dirty Dancing* 51–100 times.

July 2008 (written interview) and December 2007 (letter).

What year did you first see *Dirty Dancing*? Did someone tell you about the movie or did you just happen to hear about it?

1995. I have never seen *Dirty Dancing* on the cinema screen. I wish I had. My son bought me the video for my birthday. I watched it so many times that I wore it out and had to buy another one.

Why do you like *Dirty Dancing* so much?

I think it is a film that makes you feel good. I love it.

How has *Dirty Dancing* impacted you personally? Doreen wrote this letter to me on December 16, 2007:

I will always be a fan of Patrick's. It might sound fanciful but in a way being a fan saved my life. I was very overweight in 1995 when I saw *Dirty Dancing*. I was an instant fan. I thought that one day I might meet Patrick so I would not want to meet him looking so fat, so I dieted and lost 2 stone in weight. Then a few months later, I had a heart attack. If I had not lost that weight, I might have died. So I will always be a fan of Patrick's.

Until I saw *Dirty Dancing*, I did not know about Patrick. I had seen him in *North and South* on TV—did not know his name then.

In addition to *Dirty Dancing*, what are the names of movies that you have seen multiple times, and is Patrick in them?

I have all of Patrick's films and TV series on DVD and watch them time after time.

Have you ever met Patrick or anyone from the cast?

I have never met him. I wish I had.

Will you continue to watch *Dirty Dancing*?

Yes.

What do you think about *Dirty Dancing,* the movie being made into the stage production, and do you plan on seeing it?

I will not see it. It is on in London, not where I live.

Do you think a good sequel to the movie could be made?

No. Nothing would be right. I agree with Patrick. He says it can't be done.

Do you know other people your age who watch the movie?

Yes, lots of friends and family. Also, my pen friend Elenore, who I met through the fan club.

Anything else you want to say about *Dirty Dancing*?

It is a great film. It makes you happy to see it and the music is fantastic.

Additional Demographic Information

Marital status: Married

Education: Secondary modern

Occupation: Retired

Official Patrick Swayze International Fan Club member: Yes, 1995

ROBERTA TESKA

Age 83. Lives in Lake Worth, Florida.

March 18, 2009 (telephone interview).

Has seen *Dirty Dancing* approximately 51–100 times.

What year did you first see *Dirty Dancing*?

1988.

How old were you?

Sixty-three.

How did you hear about *Dirty Dancing*? Did someone tell you about the movie?

I think I that I was visiting up north-my son . . . Whether it came on TV or they had the video, I don't remember, but that's the first time I saw it. I had never ever seen *North and South*. I didn't really know Patrick at that point in time.

How many times have you seen *Dirty Dancing*?

It is so hard to say, I'll just go with the middle, 51–100 times. Honestly, it is impossible to give that answer. The only time I saw it up on the big screen was when I went for the Swayze reunion . . . To this day, almost every day, you'll see it somewhere on TV. It's still being shown constantly. It just never died.

Why do you like *Dirty Dancing* so much?

It's Patrick's dancing. In all honesty, it wasn't the story, which may not be what you want to hear . . . What blew my mind was Patrick's dancing. I have seen Russian ballet dancers . . . I have never seen anyone move the way he does in that movie when he is dancing. Every single little itsy bitsy part of him moves . . . if you really look, especially that scene when she goes with him to that gig.

At the Sheldrake?

Yes, it shows up so plainly. Also, it was him like when she was carrying the watermelon. He comes over with this finger crooking . . . beckoning with one finger, and the look on his face and the body language. Just everything about that was so unique. He used that in some other movie. I can't remember what movie that was . . . Everything about him in that movie. I happen to be very big on body language in acting. Peter Coyote, we've became very dear friends, ever since 1991 . . . He is a remarkable actor. He is a chameleon. He absolutely becomes another person . . . there are not too many actors that do that. What grabbed me very much with Patrick was his body language in that role. He was very good . . . What got me was Patrick, himself, his dancing in particular and especially when he was dancing with Penny. That first time when he comes in . . . when the two of them are dancing . . . They were supposed to be doing their job as instructors . . . When they first start—the two of them—down an aisle between people and just the way they are moving in toward each other—sort of a walking dance . . . Just everything about the way he dances—his body language and in the acting in the movie itself. It was excellent . . . It was really, really good. I've never seen anyone move like that . . . and it is particularly evident at The Sheldrake—although it also shows up in that final dance scene— when he comes off the stage. It's gorgeous. That was beautifully done.

I also liked the music very much—especially "She's Like The Wind."

How has *Dirty Dancing* impacted you personally?

I had sent Patrick a birthday card years ago, you know, through the fan club . . . I mean the man is incredible. He really is . . . My feelings don't have so much to do with DD but as with Patrick and Lisa. And when I sent that birthday card . . . part of it was how much he had brought into my life—that I had been a loner most of my life . . . even in high school. Because of my interest in Patrick, I found Swayze Mania and the fan club. And I have wonderful friends now since I discovered him and started searching. I have friends throughout the states—very, very good friends . . . We will e-mail off list. We call each other. There is a true friendship, and I said Patrick, I would not have this if you weren't you. And that's the god honest truth. I have the most wonderful friend . . . We have been very close. I was so happy she was in Houston and I was able to meet her in person. I mean we'll get on the phone maybe two hours.

Doesn't she live in England?

Yes, she does live in England. She has been the most wonderful friend to me. We are very close. Also, my friend in Canada—I got to meet her in Houston, and Sandy her guide dog. We are very close. What I got out of that was so remarkable—not only did I meet Patrick in person when we went to Houston—and Lisa, and his mom, Patsy, but so many of my wonderful friends that have become so dear to me—that have brought so much into my life.

I wanted him to know how much he, just simply by being, brought into my life. And also in an anniversary card, I wrote to Patrick and Lisa how their togetherness, as they have the kind of togetherness, it's very obvious . . . he's on location, she's there . . . It's the kind of togetherness that I had with my husband. So even though I had lost my husband more than twenty years ago, it just gave me such a warm feeling to see it with them. It's very evident how he wants her with him . . . I just admire them and love that much more because it brings that back in my life through them. That's how much the two of them really have brought.

I like his acting, the dancing. The more I learned, the more I felt something about him that led me to his interview with Barbara Walters. His emotional response to her question about his dad showed a quality to him that made me search more and more about him and his life —and then my interest extended to Lisa as well. As you see, *Dirty Dancing* is what brought him and Lisa into my life in a way that's impacted it tremendously. But it's them—not the movie—them as a couple . . .

Are there other movies that you have seen many times, and if so, is Patrick in them?

There are many other non-Patrick movies that I have watched through the years multiple times and many of Patrick's as well, but none as many times as *Dirty Dancing*. I love *Waking Up in Reno*. I love him with Melanie Griffith—oh my god that scene—the one you know where they made the trip to find his son, and you know, he's done some really good stuff . . . To me, one of the finest bits of acting he did. I absolutely love *Father Hood*. One spot in that movie was just brilliant—in that one scene in the courtroom. I get on the verge of tears just picturing it . . . He finally opens up and he is not giving a line. And you can see in the movie too when he began to really care about them. He did beautiful, beautiful acting. It is funny and delightful but more than that, he did a damned good job of acting . . . It was an Oscar moment . . . he knew that this man was going to be dead—his buddy. He comes in and he's talking to him and he rolls him over and he sees the knife in him [*Road House*]. There was an incredible piece of Patrick's acting in each of these two movies . . . I also loved the one where he had run away from home and came back . . .

***Tiger Warsaw*?**

Yes, I guess he was in his dressing room . . . his dog was with him . . . He said that role was killing him—what he had to feel—what he had to go through . . . this is one where he had the thing with his father . . . so he had lost that father . . . so I am sure he drew on his feelings for his own father. He has done some awfully good work. He really has. There are many others . . . *Dirty Dancing* is the one that I have watched the most. There were some I did not care for. That dark, dark movie.

***Donnie Darko*?**

Yes, I am not saying that he did not do good acting. I just didn't like the movie.

***City of Joy*?**

It was good. He has said that *City of Joy* affected him personally very deeply. He has said that *City of Joy* affected his personal life.

Have you ever met Patrick or anyone else from the cast?

You know the answer.

What was it like?

It [Houston International Film Festival—premiere of *One Last Dance*, 2003] was incredible—it really, really was. It was the most incredible experience. First of all, to be that close to Patrick and Lisa. You know, to be able to hear them . . . First, the movie, *One Last Dance*, moved me hugely. She did an utterly incredible job with that movie. She personally—with the directing and everything else. She did an incredible job. It left me breathless. I was so moved by that movie. And then, to have the opportunity . . . Patrick spent so much time with us [the fan club members] . . . He set up an area for us . . . were you there?

Yes, but I want you to tell it.

He spent so much time for us. He was so caring. He deliberately set aside an area for our group. I probably have you up on my wall because I have the picture that was taken with Patrick. There was the bus driver who was a classmate of his. It was a remarkable experience. What was more so even was the next morning. We had no idea. Margaret [President of the fan club] had no idea. She went upstairs because she had to go over something with Patrick.

Well, I only know that the first we knew anything . . . Patsy came down to tell us that he would be down. We were all wondering, "What are we sitting here for?" (***The group of about thirty fans, including Roberta and myself, were sitting on a bus in front of the hotel that Patrick and Lisa were staying at—waiting to go on a tour. As a surprise, Patrick and his mother, Patsy, came on the bus and answered any questions we had for them for about fifty minutes.***)

I just happened to be sitting in the third row, and did eventually

manage to get a question out to Patrick, which he and Patsy answered in great detail.

The way he was with us. The way he was just so down-to-earth and caring and one-on-one with each one of us.

Exactly.

That's a very rare quality. He has impacted my life in many, many, many ways. And now of course, I send prayers up to him and Lisa . . . Let's not get into that . . . can't handle *Dirty Dancing* now. It's on almost every night—on one channel or another . . . I can't handle any of his work right now . . .

What do you think about *Dirty Dancing,* the movie being made into a stage production? Do you plan on seeing it?

I am not interested. I would not see it. Of course, Eleanor Bergstein is connected with the stage production. When they were going to do a remake of *Dirty Dancing*, they were not going to use any of the people Patrick cared about, so he wasn't interested. For me, *Dirty Dancing* is Patrick. I don't believe that there is any other person who could ever, ever, ever move in the way that Patrick does. It would not satisfy me to see somebody else in the role . . . I love Baryshnikov and Nureyev. They don't move that way . . . No, I would not ever. In fact, I resented the other stupid thing that they used *Dirty Dancing* in . . .

Havana Nights.

They used the story. She had a sister . . . Javier wasn't approved by her family . . . And then they had them doing the three together. There are so many pieces that they took out of that movie and transferred into *Havana Nights*—copying it. It was horrible . . . I went to it only because Patrick was going to be onscreen for a period of time.

Do you think a good sequel to the movie could be made?

A great big no—underlined. Especially now given Patrick's health, but I never did feel it could be done successfully since it was the concept of the story itself that was the movie shaker of the audience response. It cannot be duplicated.

Additional demographic information

Marital status: Widow

Education level: High school graduate

Occupation: Retired

Official Patrick Swayze International Fan Club member: Not a member right now.

Anything else about *Dirty Dancing*?

I absolutely loved him with Cynthia Rhodes (Penny). She's no longer in acting. They left me speechless. I mean my jaw dropped down. I absolutely loved that. Any dancing they did together was absolutely exquisite. They were paired so perfectly. She was remarkable. I absolutely couldn't get enough of it. I wish they had done more . . . I loved her in it. I thought she was a very good actress as well as a wonderful dancer. I loved the way she spoke to Baby—when Baby said she knows Robbie has money and will help—told Baby to go back to her playpen . . . Just the way she did it. It was beautifully done . . . She is good. I can't believe, my god, the shape on her—how anybody could have such a tiny, tiny waist . . . What I loved so much—dancing meant a lot to me all the way through—and that final scene of course, at that time, I didn't know about his bad knee. That must have been horrendously painful—for him to jump off that stage . . . Knowing his history afterwards, I shudder when he jumps off the stage in that final scene. It's wonderful, it's dramatic, but it had to hurt like hell. In fact, in *Dirty Dancing* he fell off that log when he was showing her how to balance on that log. He fell a couple of times. They took him to the emergency room—that's his work ethic—that he came back and finished the scene . . . He's a remarkable man . . . He wouldn't have stunt doubles . . .

Six

SUMMARY OF THE FAN INTERVIEWS

During the interviews, I heard over and over again that there are key important reasons why people like *Dirty Dancing* so much and why this movie has had such a positive, strong impact on them. I list these reasons in no particular order:

1. The artistry of the movie

2. Patrick Swayze

3. The love story

4. The haven

5. The messages

6. The timeframe—1963

7. The inspiration to dance

8. The overall feel-good effect

First of all, there is the artistry of the movie. People love the story line, the acting of the entire cast (especially between Jennifer Grey and Patrick Swayze), the dancing/choreography, and the music. People who were interviewed said over and over again how great the individual above pieces were and how well they all fit together! Crystal (age 53) from the US said,

"I fell in love with the entire cast. Baby, Johnny, the dancers—the casting was perfect." People commented that the movie seemed real and that they could identify with the characters of Baby and Johnny. Elly (age 17) from Australia said, "I can relate to the movie in so many ways, such as being seventeen and individuating in your own unique way." She stated that Jennifer Grey's portrayal of Baby gave her strength and power to stand up for herself and for what she truly believes in. Elly also related that she really looks up to Jennifer Grey and Patrick Swayze for their performances— especially their creation of a soul connection between the characters. Kelly (age 37) from the US stated, "Jennifer Grey definitely stole the show for me . . . the character (Baby) being quirky and naïve . . . and timid . . . and then confident towards the end." Regarding the character of Johnny, David (age 52) from the US said that he identified with Johnny's initial display of a "hot-headed personality" and "victim" outlook in life, and changed these characteristics in himself and became more mature. Both David and Cheryl (age 55) from the US commented that the character of Johnny is realistic in terms of how he had to prove to himself that he was worthy—that men (per David) and people in general (per Cheryl) have a need to prove something to his or her self.

Speaking of Johnny, Patrick Swayze is mentioned over and over again. Some people went to the movie because they were already a big fan of Patrick Swayze—especially from *North and South*. Debbie (age 54) from the US: "I went to see it because I loved Patrick Swayze." Clare (age 26) from the UK said that she was so enamored with Patrick Swayze after first seeing him in *Dirty Dancing* at age six, she promised her dad that when she was older, she was going to go to America and meet Patrick Swayze (ended up meeting him in London in 2006). Roberta (age 83) from the US told me that it is Patrick's dancing that makes the movie for her—that she has never seen anyone (including the Russian ballet dancers) who can move the way he does in that movie when he is dancing. Angela (age 34) from the US commented that one of the reasons she likes the movie so much is because Patrick Swayze stars in it, and she wishes Patrick could teach her how to dance. Flabia (age 41) from Argentina wrote that as soon as she saw *Dirty Dancing* for the first time at age 23 with her cousin: "Both of us fell in love with Patrick that very moment." Becky (age 36) from the US told me that she became a fan of Patrick when she saw *North and South*— "He captured me then, and he's had me captured ever since." Kelly said one of the reasons she enjoys *Dirty Dancing* so much is " . . . because of Patrick Swayze. I always liked him. He's hot and just a good guy." Barbara S. (age 41) from Germany said, "I love Patrick, and it is a big dream of mine to dance with him." Evelyn (age 73) from the US remarked how Patrick is absolutely adorable and a perfectionist in the movie. Kari (age 51) from the US commented about the amazing talent of Patrick Swayze, and said, "He was sexy but kind, in an innocent way."

Continuing about Patrick, Roberta remarked how incredible it was that Patrick returned to work so soon after falling off of the log (scene where Johnny is teaching Baby to dance) and having had to go to the hospital for treatment of his knee, and how Patrick pulled off that jump from the stage during the finale considering his chronically painful knee. Cheryl commented about Patrick in the '80s (although this was said in regards to *Without A Word*, it can be applied to *Dirty Dancing* as well): "He would kind of limp around and be in pain and then go out on stage and perform as though nothing was wrong. I always wondered where he got the strength to do it. But that's passion—you know that driving force that we all have deep within us."

People really got in to the love story. Helena (age 24) from Greece said, "It is the ultimate love story . . . the best thing about this movie is that you see this love as it grows . . . and you become part of it . . . This movie makes me believe that there is still hope for every person to find the love of their life . . . it is keeping our faith in love strong and everlasting." Per Mallory (age 60) from the US: "It is a pure love story." Per Angela: "It made me think that maybe I could have something like that when I got older (was fourteen when she started watching *Dirty Dancing* and is now happily married to the man of her dreams). Callie (age 57) from the US commented, "There are many reasons I like the movie. Mostly the love story between two opposites as in Romeo and Juliet . . . I identified with it due to my own love story with my husband, David." (They have been married twenty-five years.) Flabia said, "In such a controversial and material world, the role of love is worth to be mentioned. I love the kind of men that have the guts to fight for love."

What I am calling the haven is also referred to by the interviewees as: an escape, a place where I feel safe, and a lifeline. Becky said, "*North and South* and *Dirty Dancing* have been escapes for me . . . they've been havens . . . It's kind of like a favorite food, or a blanket or a cup of hot chocolate . . . And he (Patrick) has helped create those places through his art—just to watch him dance." Crystal stated, "*Dirty Dancing* takes me to a place away from life's problems and takes me to a place that I feel safe . . . It helped me through my cancer treatment." Debbie wrote, " . . . because of the way *Dirty Dancing* made me feel, it helped me through a very terrible personal health ordeal, during which I almost died . . . when I was in the theater, I could smile and feel good, safe and healthy for a few hours. The movie really became a kind of lifeline for me." Evelyn said, "I was in a low period, and it upped my spirit and mood." The movie also helped two people—Mallory and Doreen (age 75) from UK—lose a significant amount of weight. Doreen commented that it may have saved her life as the weight loss helped her deal with a cardiac problem. Lelia (age 30) from Romania said, " . . . when I am feeling lonely, I just love to stay in bed and enjoy this wonderful film." Angela stated, "I had a difficult childhood, and when I would turn on the VCR, I instantly stepped into Johnny and Baby's world. It kept me together."

The messages category touches on values, ethics, and ways one can live life in a positive manner. Callie said, "It fortified my resolve that I will always do the right thing." Barbara P. (age 62) from the US talked about Baby standing up for Johnny because she knew that he did not steal the billfold. She said, "Baby stood up for what is right. Americans are losing their morals. We need some heroes . . . It's the kind of ethics that you want to instill in your kids. Johnny worked hard and had good ethics. It also shows that learning new things can be fun." Kelly said, "I think in the end, it showed people are about doing the right thing." Clare stated, "I think the film shows you that we are all different people from different backgrounds but at the same time we can all learn something from one another . . . People can sometimes make themselves come across as something they are not in order to protect themselves. I think it teaches and makes you realize never to judge people without knowing them." Kari also talked about how "'Bad boys' aren't really bad. It's a mask they wear . . . If you get beyond the facade, you will find sincerity, compassion, and also many hard knocks." Elly, Flabia, and Barbara S. all made comments about how *Dirty Dancing* has given them motivation and courage to stand up for their beliefs and feelings and to fight for what they want. Barbara S.: "I had to become forty-one years old to tell my parents my point of view, not accepting bad compromises. And now I feel comfortable with my decision." Finally, most everyone talked about the message to follow your dreams. Roy (age 35) from US said, "Dreams can come true." Mallory stated, "The movie is a positive statement of possibilities." Clare noted, "Dreams really do come true." Per Kari: "The movie gives the person the feeling that you can be anything you want to be."

Regarding the timeframe—1963, Cheryl wrote, "It reminded me of things from my past. It took me back to a time and place where things were simpler." Mallory commented that the movie resonated so much with her because: "It was the timeframe. It was 1963 . . . I also come from a Jewish family and Mountain Lake looked just like the Catskills . . . I've lived that . . . I worked in the Catskills . . . in college." Crystal said, "I remember the era. I was too young to be part of it, so *Dirty Dancing* let me live vicariously. It is an age before our world view became more cynical." Barbara P. commented that it was a less stressful time.

The next category—inspiration to dance: "After all, *Dirty Dancing* is exactly why I started to dance in the first place. It's my passion and long term commitment," said Elly. Barbara S. stated, "I re-discovered my love for dancing . . . The dancing of Patrick and others inspired me to find my own way of dancing." Kari noted that the movie inspired her to take more dance lessons, to be freer in movement and more confident in her dancing, and "to enjoy the beauty of dancing in all forms."

I saved the overall feel-good effect of the movie for last, as it most certainly incorporates all of the above themes. Here are comments made by the interviewees:

Elly: "It has been an exhilarating experience."

Helena: "It's a lighthouse of hope . . . keeps me warm in the heart."

Clare: "I feel the film is inspiring, a feel-good film . . . leaves you with a smile on your face and a warm heart . . . "

Barbara P., Roy, and Doreen: "It made me feel good."

Kelly: "It's a positive movie . . . This is an uplifting movie."

Kari: "There is so much out there to enjoy and experience if we allow ourselves the opportunity to be free. Everyone should be able to 'dance' and be 'like the wind.'"

Crystal: "*Dirty Dancing* and Patrick Swayze bring happiness. They are a happy jinx."

I will close with statements by Simone (age 35) from Germany, and Becky, that I am sure are true for many of the interviewees—Simone: "*Dirty Dancing* is a part of me," and Becky: "Patrick and *Dirty Dancing* and *North and South* are just part of who I am."

Elly Ali. Melbourne, Australia.
"It's exactly why I started dancing in the first place . . . I especially love how Patrick Swayze and Jennifer Grey can work together in such a natural, sexy, and trusting way . . . Made me realize that I can get out there and do what I love and not let anyone stop me . . . "

Helena Damigou. Athens, Greece.
"You see this love as it grows and you become part of it . . . it's really a lighthouse of hope that is shimmering in our hearts and that is keeping our faith in love strong and everlasting."

Clare Gregan. Preston, England.
" . . . standing in front of me (at the stage door) was Patrick Swayze . . . looking right back at me, Clare Gregan, the girl with a dream from nineteen years ago . . . so you see, dreams really do come true . . . inspiring, feel-good film . . . great love story . . ."

Credit: Sue Tabashnik

Becky Williams. Macomb, Michigan.
"They (Baby & Johnny) could live in the moment . . . Both *North and South* and *Dirty Dancing* have been escapes for me . . . they've been havens . . . Patrick and *Dirty Dancing* and *North and South* are just part of who I am."

Kelly Miner. Southfield, Michigan.
"Jennifer Grey definitely stole the show for me . . . the character (Baby) being quirky and naïve . . . and then confident towards the end . . . it shows love on many levels . . . happy . . . uplifting."

Barbara Schiebl. Landsburg, Germany.
"The courage of Baby inspired me to find my own courage. The dancing of Patrick and the others inspired me to find my own way of dancing . . . It's a real feel-good movie for me."

Crystal L. Berger. Birch Bay, Washington.
"I will always be grateful to Patrick Swayze and *Dirty Dancing* for helping me through this cancer . . . *Dirty Dancing* is just a gem. It has been a lovely friend for many years. Some charmed time, a little bit of sweetness."

Callie & David Van Kleeck. Glendale, Arizona.
"We BOTH love good storytelling and happy endings . . . Both Patrick and Jennifer made their characters believable. Their characters' innocence and idealistic outlook on life was genuine in them both . . . It has served as the centerpiece of MANY of our 'Date Nights' throughout our twenty-five years of marriage."

Doreen Height. Derby, England.
"It is a film that makes you feel good." She states she lost weight in case she met Patrick—then she had a heart attack, and if she hadn't lost the weight, she might have died. "So I will always be a fan of Patrick."

Roberta Teska. Lake Worth, Florida.
"What blew my mind was Patrick's dancing . . . absolutely loved him (dancing) with Cynthia Rhodes (Penny) . . . Because of my interest in Patrick, I found Swayze Mania and the fan club. And I have wonderful friends now."

I visited Patrick's star on the Hollywood Walk of Fame—7018 Hollywood Boulevard. Patrick received his star on his 45th birthday on August 18, 1997.

At the Complexions Gala in Detroit in 2004, I was lucky to have my picture taken with Sarita Allen, Artist-In-Residence, at Complexions Contemporary Ballet. Patrick (Board Member) hosted the gala for this acclaimed dance company. In addition to giving amazing, innovative, powerful performances, Complexions does outreach work with youth.

Seven

DIRTY DANCING FOLKLORE & TIDBITS

GENERAL INFORMATION

1. Eleanor Bergstein used some of her own life experiences in the story line of *Dirty Dancing.*

2. Dirty dancing really happened and was sometimes called liberated dancing or dirty dwaging.

3. The movie was initially called: *Dancing.*

4. Vestron Pictures agreed to make the movie after virtually all of the other studios had turned it down.

5. Emile Ardolino was pursued to be the director of *Dirty Dancing* because of an earlier dance documentary that he directed: *He Makes Me Feel Like Dancin'* (1983), which won an academy award for Best Documentary.

6. The movie began filming September 5, 1986 at Mountain Lake Hotel in Virginia and wrapped on October 27, 1986 at Lake Lure Inn in North Carolina.

7. The release dates were August 17, 1987—New York City premiere; August 19, 1987—LA premiere; and August 21, 1987—USA. Following the New York premiere, there was a '60s themed party at Roseland dance hall in which all the stars attended.

8. The *Dirty Dancing* TV show on CBS in fall 1988, starring Patrick Cassidy as Johnny and Melora Hardin as Baby, lasted only three months.

9. In 1988, "Dirty Dancing: Live in Concert," the musical tour, featuring Bill Medley and Eric Carmen, went to 90 cities in 90 days. (*I attended this fabulous show and to this day still have my souvenir button: "Things Go Better With *Dirty Dancing*.")

10. It was the first movie to sell 100 million video copies.

SOME *DIRTY DANCING* STARS CAME FROM SHOW BUSINESS PARENTS

1. Jennifer Grey
    Mother, Jo Wilder—actress
    Father, Joel Grey—Broadway performer
    (Grandfather, Mickey Katz—comedian—who did some performances in the Catskills)

2. Patrick Swayze
    Mother, Patsy Swayze—choreographer

3. Jerry Orbach
    Father, Leon Orbach—vaudeville
    Mother, Emily Orbach—radio singer, Broadway performer

SOME *DIRTY DANCING* STARS HAD AN EARLY START IN SHOW BUSINESS
*All five of the mentioned actors below had extensive training/experience prior to *Dirty Dancing*. This list is just some information about their very beginnings. It is not meant to be a list of all of their training/experience.

1. Patrick Swayze began dancing as a young child (as soon as he could walk) at his mother's dance studio and was in many recitals and school musicals. His first professional appearance was as a dancer in Disney on Parade, and then he appeared on Broadway in *Goodtime Charley* in 1975, and then in 1978 in *Grease* as the lead. Patrick Swayze had danced with the Houston Jazz Ballet, Harkness Ballet, Joffrey Ballet, and Eliot Feld Ballet.

2. Jennifer Grey took dancing lessons as a child but allegedly was not

allowed to perform during her childhood. She made her professional dancing and stage debut at age twenty.

3. Cynthia Rhodes danced and sang as a child and worked at Opryland as a singer and dancer at age seventeen while in high school.

4. Jerry Orbach was in many school plays and began acting in summer stock at age sixteen.

5. Kelly Bishop had her first dance job at age eighteen at Radio City Music Hall.

6. Jack Weston began acting at age ten.

SOME *DIRTY DANCING* CAST MEMBERS/CHOREOGRAPHERS WORKED TOGETHER BEFORE *DIRTY DANCING*

1. In 1969, Jerry Orbach starred on Broadway in *Promises, Promises* for which he won a Tony Award as Actor in a musical. Kelly Bishop was in the chorus.

2. In 1975, Joel Grey (Jennifer Grey's father) starred on Broadway in *Goodtime Charley* and Patrick Swayze played a dancer and servant in the same show.

3. Kenny Ortega was the choreographer for the movie, *Xanadu* (1980) which starred Olivia Newton-John and Gene Kelly. Gene Kelly became a mentor to Kenny Ortega. Cynthia Rhodes appeared as an ensemble dancer in *Xanadu,* which was her first movie role. Miranda Garrison appeared as a dancer.

4. Jennifer Grey and Patrick Swayze were featured together in the movie, *Red Dawn* in 1984.

5. Jennifer Grey was featured in the movie, *Ferris Bueller's Day Off* (1986) and Kenny Ortega was choreographer and a second-unit director.

SOME *DIRTY DANCING* CAST MEMBERS/CHOREOGRAPHERS/COMPOSERS WORKED TOGETHER AFTER *DIRTY DANCING*

1. Patrick Swayze starred in *To Wong Foo Thanks For Everything! Julie Newmar* (1995), and Kenny Ortega was the choreographer.

2. Patrick Swayze made a cameo appearance as a dance instructor, and Miranda Garrison was an assistant choreographer and dancer in the prequel movie, *Dirty Dancing: Havana Nights* (2004).

3. Kelly Bishop starred in the television show, *Gilmore Girls,* and Kenny Ortega directed some episodes.

4. Kenny Ortega and Miranda Garrison are cast members in the documentary, *MOVE* (2010).

5. Stacy Widelitz and Patrick Swayze co-wrote the song "Cliff's Edge" for *Road House* (1989) and Patrick Swayze performed it. Stacy Widelitz worked on the theatrical production of *Without A Word* in 1984 with Patrick Swayze. Stacy Widelitz composed music for *One Last Dance* (2003), which was the movie adaptation of *Without A Word*.

DIRTY DANCING CAST MEMBERS AND THEIR SHOW BUSINESS SPOUSES

1. Patrick Swayze and Lisa Niemi—writer, director, dancer, producer, actor—met at Patsy Swayze's (mother) dance studio in 1971 and were married 1975–2009. In the movie, *Grandview U. S. A.* (1984), they both were choreographers and Patrick had a lead role. They starred together in the movie, *Steel Dawn*(1987). They collaborated together for the movie, *One Last Dance* (2003). Lisa was writer, producer, lead actor, and Patrick was producer, lead actor, financier. (Also, *Without A Word*, the 1984 stage production created and starred in by Patrick, Lisa, and Nicholas Gunn from which *One Last Dance* was based, won six LA Drama Critic Awards.) Patrick starred in the TV series *The Beast* (2009) and Lisa directed one of the episodes. Patrick and Lisa danced together at the World Music Awards in 1994 (which Patrick was hosting).

2. Kelly Bishop and Lee Leonard—TV talk show host and anchor—married in 1981.

3.   Cynthia Rhodes and Richard Marx—singer, musician, writer, producer, arranger first met in connection with the movie, *Staying Alive* (1983) and married in 1989.

4.   Jennifer Grey and Clark Greg—actor, screenwriter—married in 2001.

MISCELLANEOUS INFORMATION

1.   Eleanor Bergstein was named for Eleanor Roosevelt.

2.   Eleanor Bergstein was called Baby up until age twenty-one or so, as she was the younger daughter in the family. She won dance contests as a teen and was an Arthur Murray dance instructor. Her father was a physician. She spent some vacation time with her family in the Catskills.

3.   Eleanor Bergstein made a cameo appearance in *Dirty Dancing* in the scene on the gazebo, dancing with Johnny right before he leaves to get Penny out of the kitchen.

4.   Shortly after *Dirty Dancing* was released, 25,000 posters of Patrick Swayze sold out instantly.

5.   Following the release of *Dirty Dancing*, there was an influx of people signing up for dance lessons.

6.   Patrick Swayze was named the sexiest man alive in 1991 by *People* magazine. He also wrote the introduction for the special *People* edition: *20 Years of Sexiest Man Alive*.

7.   Patrick Swayze received a star on the Hollywood Walk of Fame— 7018 Hollywood Boulevard—on August 18, 1997, which was his 45th birthday.

8.   In 1975, Jerry Orbach played Billy Flynn in the original Broadway production of *Chicago*, and in 2003, Patrick Swayze played the same role on Broadway.

9.   Jerry Orbach was inducted into the Theater Hall of Fame in 2000.

10. Charles "Honi" Coles, who played Tito in *Dirty Dancing*, was placed in

the International Tap Dance Hall of Fame in 2003.

11. Kelly Bishop won a Tony Award in 1976 for her performance in *A Chorus Line.*

12. Patrick Swayze performed in thirty-seven movies (including four TV movies) and also was nominated for a Golden Globe three times—including for *Dirty Dancing.* He was awarded Best International Actor for *Jump!* on May 16, 2009 and the Rolex Dance Award in November 2009.

13. Jennifer Grey was nominated for a Golden Globe award for *Dirty Dancing.*

14. "She's Like The Wind" was originally written for the movie, *Grandview U. S. A.* (1984) by Stacy Widelitz and Patrick Swayze.

15. Kenny Ortega has won many awards, including two ALMA (American Latino Media Arts Award), three Primetime Emmys, and three American Choreography Awards.

*Note: *Dirty Dancing* Folklore & Tidbits is not meant to be by any means a complete list of all of the experience, accomplishments, and talents of the amazing *Dirty Dancing* Writer/Cast Members/Producers/Choreographers/ Composers, etc.

Eight

SUE'S *DIRTY DANCING* QUESTIONNAIRE

Dirty Dancing Questionnaire

1. Rate the movie *Dirty Dancing* on a scale from 1–10 (10 is highest rating)

1 ▾

2. How many times have you seen *Dirty Dancing*?

0 ▾

3. When is the last time that you saw *Dirty Dancing*?

today ▾

4. Choose your 3 favorite scenes in *Dirty Dancing*

☐ Finale dance scene

☐ Water lift scene

☐ Penny and Johnny teaching Baby how to dance, Johnny says: "spaghetti arms"

☐ Baby giggling while Johnny is putting his hand down her arm

☐ When Baby says to Johnny: "I carried a watermelon"

☐ When Johnny dances with Baby for the first time in the staff room

☐ When Johnny is teaching Baby to feel the music and puts their hands on his heart

☐ other

Other—please tell me your other favorite scenes

5. Choose up to 5 things you like best about *Dirty Dancing*.

☐ the love story

☐ the dancing

☐ the music

☐ the acting

☐ Jennifer Grey

☐ Patrick Swayze

☐ the coming of age story

☐ the overcoming of class story

☐ the story takes place in the '60s

☐ other

Other—please tell me the other things you like best

6. Choose the top 4 reasons why you think *Dirty Dancing* has remained popular for over 20 years

☐ the love story

☐ the coming of age story

☐ the feel good story

☐ the acting

☐ the dancing and music

☐ the story takes place in a more innocent time

☐ the self-discovery of the characters

☐ the value of integrity

☐ the characters seem real and you feel for them

☐ other

Other—please tell me your other reasons

7. In what ways has *Dirty Dancing* had a positive impact on your life?

☐ has provided worthwhile entertainment

☐ has provided relief in a difficult time

☐ has given hope that love exists

☐ has been an emotional catharsis

☐ has given hope that people will do the right thing

☐ N/A

☐ other

Other — please tell me any other positive impact

[text box]

DATE [   ]

NAME(Optional) [   ]

AGE [5 - 10 ▼]

MALE OR FEMALE ☐ Male ☐ Female

COUNTRY [   ]

RACE(optional) [   ]

E- MAIL ADDRESS AND/OR PHONE NUMBER (If interested in being contacted for an interview)

[text box]

Submit | Reset

I would like to interview people who have been positively influenced by the movie. I hope to publish the results and analysis of the survey and interviews, along with other information about *Dirty Dancing* to honor the movie and the fans' perspective on the movie.

Sue Tabashnik © Copyright 2007

QUESTIONNAIRE RESULTS

The questionnaire was placed online on November 25, 2007, and questionnaires were accepted through August 30, 2008. The total number of questionnaires received was 186. The following pages will display questionnaire results that include data by age and country; answers to questions 1, 4, 6, and 7; and comments from the fans on questions 4, 5, 6, and 7.

Credits:
Compilation of data:
Sue Tabashnik

Initial formatting of data:
Margaret Howden

Final formatting of data:
Jan Griffith

AGE	Male	Female	Total
4 to 10	0	1	1
11 to 17	0	5	5
18 to 30	2	38	40
31 to 50	6	73	79
51 to 65	8	38	46
66 to 80	1	12	13
81 +	0	1	1
No answer	0	1	1
Totals	17	169	186

AGES OF FANS

Number of Fans

Legend:
- 4 - 10
- 11 - 17
- 18 - 30
- 31 - 50
- 51 - 65
- 66 - 80
- 81 +
- No answer

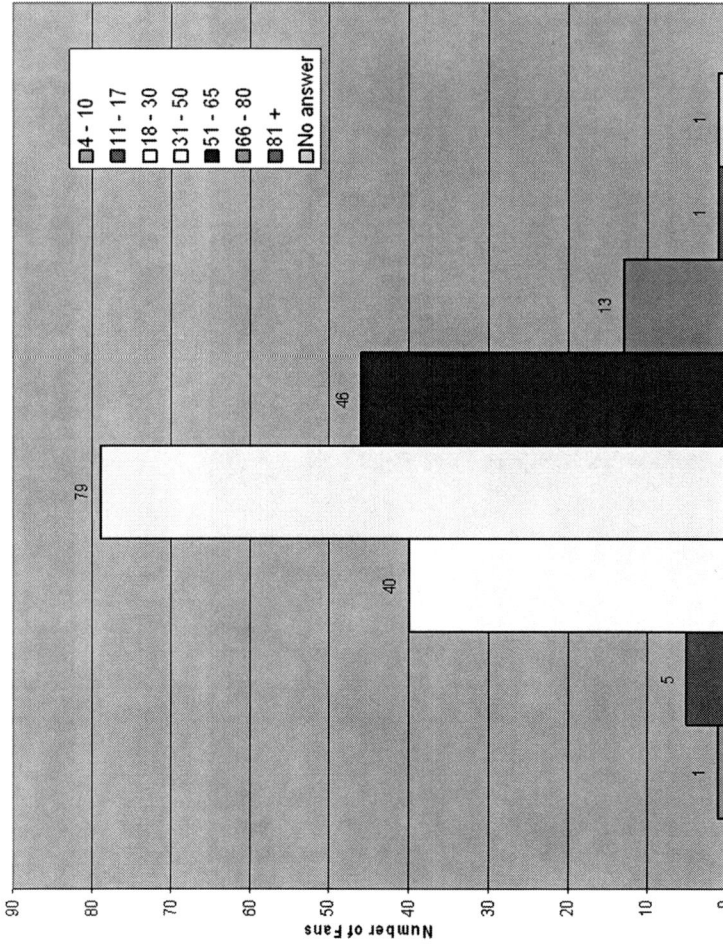

NUMBER OF FANS WHO COMPLETED SURVEY BY COUNTRY

Number of fans

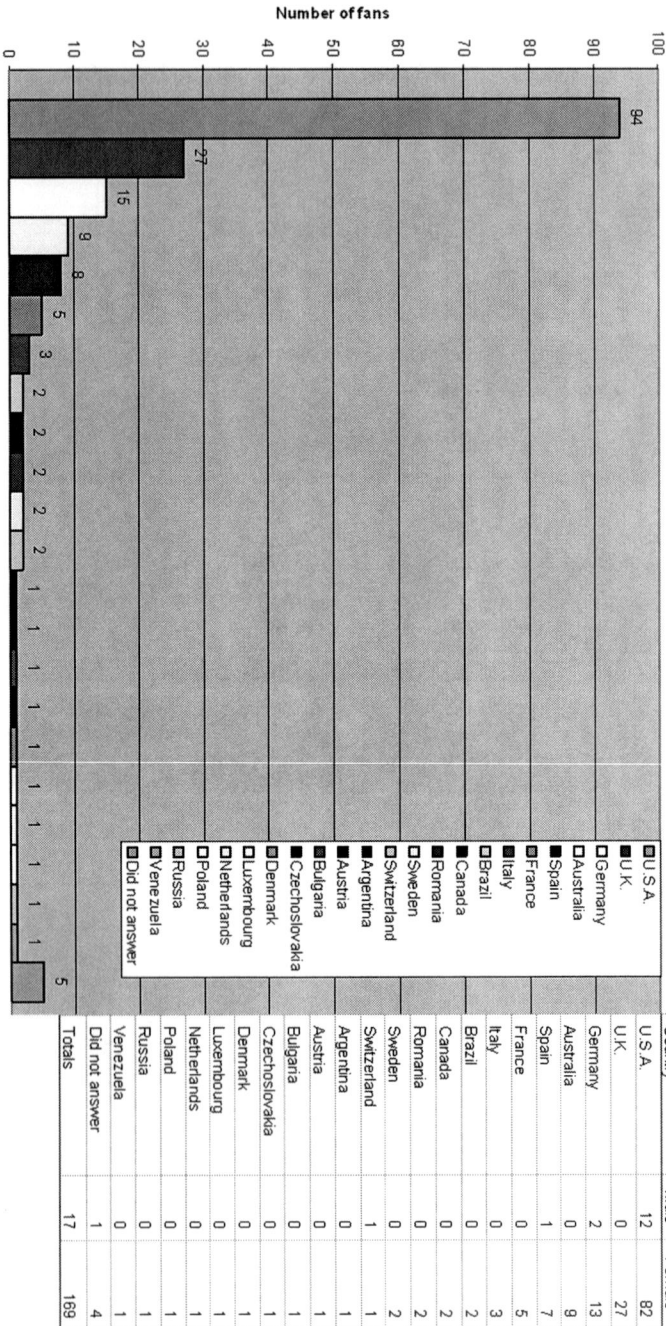

Country	Male	Female
U.S.A.	12	82
U.K.	0	27
Germany	2	13
Australia	0	9
Spain	1	7
France	0	5
Italy	0	3
Brazil	0	2
Canada	0	2
Romania	0	2
Sweden	0	2
Switzerland	1	1
Argentina	0	1
Austria	0	1
Bulgaria	0	1
Czechoslovakia	0	1
Denmark	0	1
Luxembourg	0	1
Netherlands	0	1
Poland	0	1
Russia	0	1
Venezuela	0	1
Did not answer	1	4
Totals	17	169

QUESTION 1:
RATE THE MOVIE ON A SCALE FROM 1 TO 10
^10 is the highest rating
^^No votes lower than 5

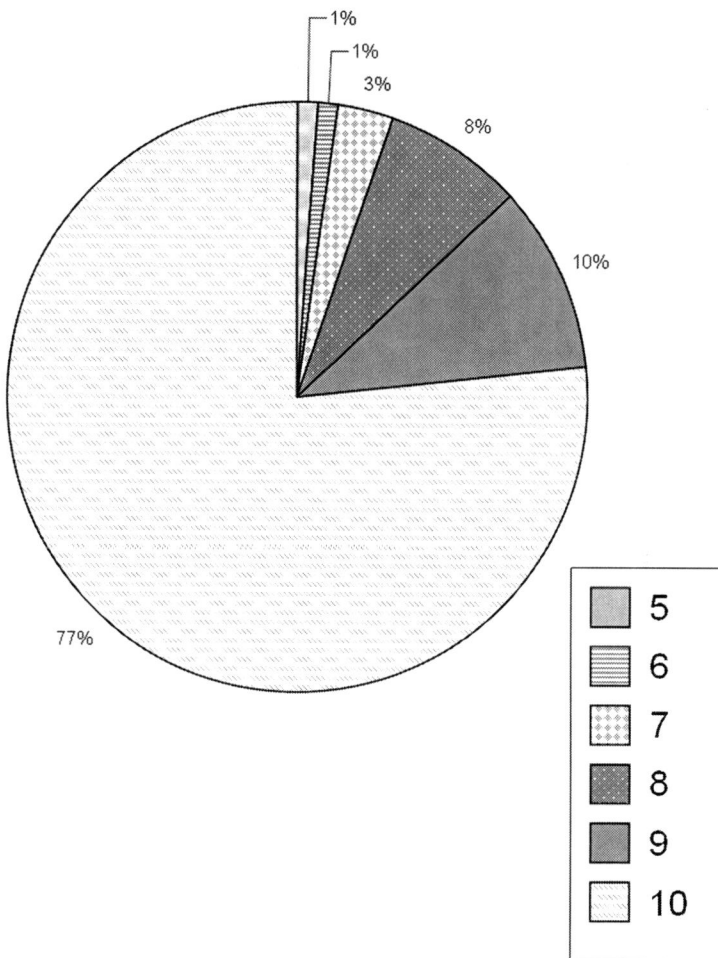

1%
1%
3%
8%
10%
77%

	5
	6
	7
	8
	9
	10

QUESTION 4:
CHOOSE YOUR 3 FAVORITE SCENES IN *DIRTY DANCING*

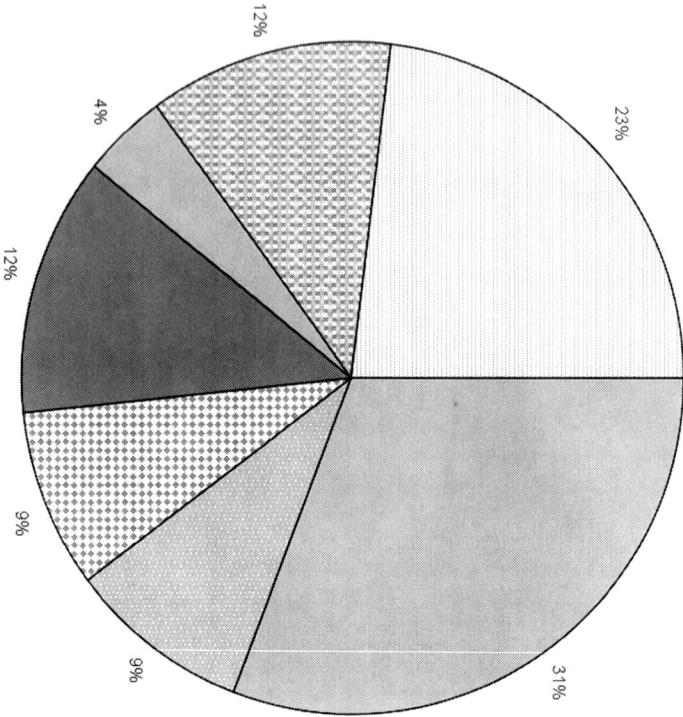

23%

12%

4%

12%

9%

9%

31%

☑ Finale dance scene

☑ Water lift scene

☐ Penny and Johnny teaching Baby how to dance, Johnny says "spaghetti arms"

◼ Baby giggling while Johnny is putting his hand down her arm

☐ Baby says to Johnny: "I carried a watermelon"

☐ Johnny dances with Baby for the first time in the staff room

☐ Johnny teaching Baby to dance and puts their hands on his heart

QUESTION 6:
CHOOSE THE TOP 4 REASONS WHY YOU THINK *DIRTY DANCING* HAS REMAINED POPULAR OVER 20 YEARS

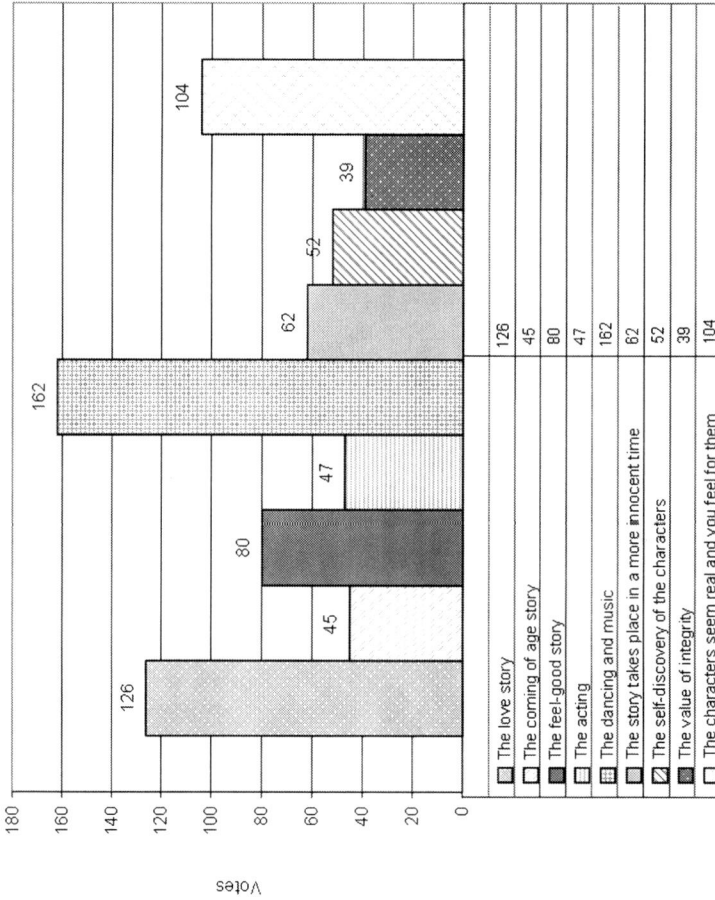

	Votes
The love story	126
The coming of age story	45
The feel-good story	80
The acting	47
The dancing and music	162
The story takes place in a more innocent time	62
The self-discovery of the characters	52
The value of integrity	39
The characters seem real and you feel for them	104

QUESTION 7:
IN WHAT WAYS HAS *DIRTY DANCING* HAD A POSITIVE IMPACT ON YOUR LIFE?

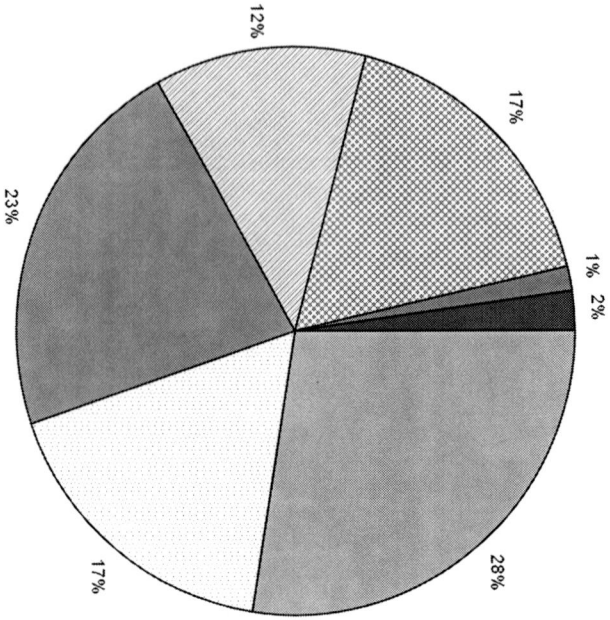

	Male	Female	Total	%
▨ Has provided worthwhile entertainment	10	97	107	28
▨ Has provided relief in a difficult time	2	66	68	17
▨ Has given hope that love exists	7	80	87	23
▨ Has been an emotional catharsis	1	47	48	12
▨ Has given hope people will do the right thing	7	60	67	17
▨ N/A	1	4	5	1
▨ #7 not on the questionnaire	1	8	9	2
Totals	29	362	391	100

QUESTION 4: CHOOSE YOUR FAVORITE SCENES IN *DIRTY DANCING*—OTHER:

Please tell me your other favorite scenes.

***Number written before the comment indicates how many people made the comment.**

36: When Baby goes to Johnny's room after Penny's abortion and Baby's father snubbed Johnny. Baby and Johnny dance in Johnny's room and Baby says, "I'm scared of everything . . . most of all I'm scared of walking out of this room and never feeling for the rest of my life the way I feel when I am with you."

5: Johnny and Baby singing "Hey Baby" in the studio—the Sylvia and Mickey scene.

3: Johnny and Baby dancing the Mambo at The Sheldrake. Its awkwardness is endearing and very well-filmed—realistic, entertaining, and funny.

3: After Johnny and Baby danced in the hotel and return by car, when Johnny looks in the mirror while Baby is changing her clothes. I love the smile on his face.

3: When Baby and Johnny are in Penny's room. Baby leaves, then Johnny follows seconds later. Baby is standing on the deck, and they say some wonderful things. Johnny walks away. Then Baby yells, "Johnny," and he turns around and makes this wonderful smile.

3: Baby's conversations with her father—when asking for the money for the abortion and when they reconcile over it.

2: Johnny and Penny doing the first dance—the mambo.

2: When Johnny has to leave and says goodbye to Baby and the song, "She's Like The Wind" is playing while he is driving away.

2: Outside of the movie, more particularly the extras. I really enjoyed seeing and experiencing the learning curve of Johnny and Baby for the various sequences. I am a dancer myself and loved this a lot.

2: When Johnny, Penny, Baby, and Billy meet to find a solution.

2: When Johnny fights with Robbie.

2: All scenes.

2: When Baby's father told Johnny he was sorry.

2: When Baby sees Johnny for the first time.

1: When Billy takes Baby to the hall where the Dirty Dancers are and soon Johnny & Penny go bouncing in and do their dancing.

1: I luv this movie, so much. I watch it constantly. I grew up with this movie. It is one of my favorites.

1: When Baby finds money and gives it to Penny.

1: Almost the whole movie is wonderful.

1: It's hard to pick just one scene, but just looking at Patrick gets this sixty-six year old married granny's heart pumping.

1: It brings back the memory of your first time you fell for a boy . . . brings back memories of a sock hop . . . It was a big deal to get asked to dance.

1: When her sister does the hula thing.

1: When she tells him her real name.

1: After the Schumakers get caught stealing and Johnny comes to find Baby in the staff quarters. He tells her that he's done, and she gets upset because what she did was not good enough to save him. Johnny basically tells Baby not to lose faith in life and that he has learned to have faith through her.

1: When Johnny takes responsibility for Penny's situation.

QUESTION 5: CHOOSE UP TO 5 THINGS YOU LIKE BEST ABOUT *DIRTY DANCING*—OTHER:

Please tell me the other things that you liked best.

*2 similar comments: Everything. This movie is excellent, how Jen portrays a teen, how she falls for the hot Patrick. The dancing, acting, music, the entire movie. Also, the love scenes.

The randomness of it. To clarify, I always thought, even at age six when I first saw it, that Baby and Johnny were not meant to be. It makes the story bittersweet, and conveys a "make the most out of the moments you're given in life, even if circumstances are not optimal" type message.

Baby and Johnny get people to change their minds.

Choreography.

It gives hope.

The courage Baby has to love Johnny against the will of her father.

The first dance with Penny is very, very good.

In the beginning, Johnny was so sarcastic towards Baby, but how he begins to soften up towards her.

You can actually go to Mountain Lake and be where the movie was filmed. I did that and will never forget it. I stood where Patrick Swayze stood. My favorite memory was the feeling I got when I was there.

Johnny teaching Baby to dance in turn brings out a talent that she would have never known that she had. Sometimes you do not know what you have until someone else brings it out in you.

How we need to learn to trust our teenagers and spend more time with them than we did in the '60s.

The feel-good feeling that comes when I watch the movie.

I also enjoyed Orbach's role. I also loved his acting.

"Nobody puts Baby in the corner." My grandchildren love that movie also—
thirteen year old and ten year old.

The beauty of the location.

For a love story, it kept me on the edge of my seat every time. I just wanted
the movie to never end.

I'm from the '60s and vividly remember dirty dancing . . . it made us feel
alive, and like we could do anything!!! This movie takes me right back to the
scenarios in my own life. I love it all!!!

As it is my favorite movie ever, I really love Jennifer Grey's natural talent and
Patrick Swayze guiding her to be the best she can be as she also brings out
the best in him.

It is very sexy.

'57 Chevy. How can I find out what happened to it?

The love story.

The dancing is smooth and phenomenal. It taught me that in order to dance
with a partner, you have to really feel the music and totally be in sync with
that person. You almost have to breathe in one another.

**QUESTION 6: CHOOSE THE TOP 4 REASONS *DIRTY DANCING* HAS
REMAINED POPULAR OVER 20 YEARS—OTHER:**

Please tell me your other reasons.

11 people wrote comments about Patrick Swayze: Patrick Swayze. Number
one on this list would have to be Patrick Swayze . . . because Patrick Swayze
is very beautiful and dances very, very good. Patrick Swayze stars in this
movie and that's why it has remained popular.

I think the way the movie was made/the way it turned out is also important.
Some movies have a "feel" to them that is special; DD is one of those movies.
It's got a charming, almost magical feel to it—with a very simple manner of
storytelling, nothing convoluted, over-earnest or over-the-top—that makes

you overlook some of its faults, and just yearn to rewatch it and relive it.

It is hard to choose just four reasons. All of these add to the popularity.

Choreography.

When Johnny is leaving, he says goodbye to Baby and "She's Like The Wind" is playing.

When Johnny goes to see Baby's Dad.

Everything about the movie is the best.

It is just a feel-good all over movie.

My kids and grandchildren can sing all the songs in the movie. It's fun.

It's a story for all ages . . . integrity and love never die, and there's something of this movie in everybody's past, whether they'll admit it or not.

It's a movie that brings two people from different sides of the tracks together, and they begin to come to terms with each other's expectations, and they could make it work as they both say "fight harder" and that's what Johnny and Baby did. They fought and overcame their fears and found trust in one another.

Every time I watch it, it is like watching it for the first time. It evokes the same feelings every time.

The acting bond the characters had with each other. They "clicked" well with each other.

It's solid. Well-choreographed and really romantic without being too over-the-top.

QUESTION 7: IN WHAT WAYS HAS *DIRTY DANCING* HAD A POSITIVE IMPACT ON YOUR LIFE?

OTHER: Please tell me any other positive impact.

Since *Dirty Dancing*, I have been a huge Patrick fan and through my Patrick Swayze message board and Perfectly Patrick fan club, I've made many friends and was able to talk to Patrick on the phone.

It's made me a dancer. I am not an entertainment professional, but I firmly believe in taking dancing, singing, and/or anything else pertaining to the arts, as it helps a great deal in getting through life, and should be something everyone delves in, whether they are professionals or not.

Following up on the story of how it was made and the impact it had on those involved in the movie. Very real people.

Joined the Patrick Swayze fan club.

Because of the actor, Patrick Swayze.

I have always thought that honesty and innocence can't be played. Either you have these qualities or you don't. It can't be faked. Patrick (Johnny) & Jen (Baby) are really (in real life) honest people with high integrity who show innocence in its finest form.

It has been a lovely friend through many years.

I'm twenty-six years old and first watched the film at just six years old. Patrick was my idol all that time. I always said to my daddy, when I'm a big girl I'm going to America and hunt him down. Well, last year my dream came true, and I finally met him and shared three months in London in his company. He saved me a huge air fare, showed me that dreams really do come true, no matter how big they are . . .

Watching *Dirty Dancing* gave me an "escape" from life as I was growing up. I had a difficult childhood, and when I would turn on the VCR, I instantly stepped into Johnny and Baby's world. It kept me together.

Has given me hope for my life, that I will have courage to find my own way, especially in dancing.

I have leave school a long time ago, and I learn English with this movie because text is easy now. I continue to learn English with speak up (magazine). Now I have many movies with Patrick, and I see them in American or English for hearing his voice with his accent. I like *One Last Dance* also. That's given me strength and willpower for making sport. Thanks to Patrick and Lisa.

Every time I hear a *Dirty Dancing* song or watch a *Dirty Dancing* advertisement just for coincidence, suddenly I feel that next activity or moment of life I am going to live will be positive and perfect. That give me motivation, charge my batteries. I am studying tourism, and I am preparing myself in language and hotel skills and hotel management, in order to reach my dream to work in Mountain Lake Hotel (Virginia).

Being introduced to Patrick Swayze and enjoying watching him in all his other movies. It has been so much fun for me to get so caught up in him, and I honestly feel like I know him just through the roles he has chosen to play.

Patrick Swayze has always been an inspiration to me in every way. *Dirty Dancing* was the movie that opened my eyes to see what a true artist he is.

I was already a Swayze fan when the movie came out, so that's why I went to see it. But WOW! I was very ILL at that time and alone. My family was thousands of miles away. I was too sick to work and very depressed. I went to the movies every day—sometimes twice a day. After the first week, I think I knew every word.

It puts you in a great mood, and it makes you want to get out there and dance the night away.

Just love it.

I believe that this movie has also made me think that there are people out there like Baby & Johnny. I also think it has made me feel like things happen when you least expect it.

That the best-looking gal didn't get the guy.

When I get depressed, this movie really cheers me up. This movie is so awesome. This movie has impacted my life totally. Patrick is such a hunk.

That love, truth, and honesty will prevail in love . . .

Patrick Swayze was the first actor I had a crush on, and he's still the one! So I finally had an idol.

That the guy can finish first place. It shows our kids that good values do count and that learning new things can be fun. Don't give up your dreams.

Always makes me happy no matter what mood I am in.

It is just a beautiful story & the best movie I have ever seen. I love to watch it.

For me, I was going through a terrible time in my life where I needed something "good" to hang on to. Something positive to focus on, and something for me to strive towards—a love like that one! (I have it!)

I listen to the music, and find myself smiling . . . can't help myself. And it introduced two great characters, Johnny and Baby, as well as actors, Patrick Swayze and Jennifer Grey, into my life.

I can relate to it in so many ways, such as being seventeen years old and breaking away and individuating in your own unique way, and me and Jennifer Grey are alike. I really look up to her in a way that has given me strength and power to stand up for myself, and stand up for what I believe in no matter if it's to dance or fall in love. I really thank her for that, and Patrick is a dream come true. They could not have picked better actors to suit this film. Those two have a great chemistry, which nobody can take away from them. It will live on forever, because nobody puts Baby and Johnny in a corner.

The movie itself has a large impact in my life. Patrick Swayze is a role model of mine from that movie alone, so I would have to say all of the above & more.

You can do whatever makes you happy.

Patrick is an equestrian in his non-acting hours, and his love for nature and horses has inspired me. It was through watching DD interviews etc. that I learned of his love for them. I ended up being a volunteer through STEP, which is a therapeutic Equestrian Program for disabled children. I have always wanted to work with horses, and he inspired me to do a good deed for children in need. This has turned out to be a very rewarding experience— not only working with children but also with horses.

It still inspires me that a person can really fulfill their dreams if they put their heart and mind to it.

I saw the movie when I was twelve and now am thirty-three. At that time and still now, sexy Johnny, that came from a different class, fights for his place in the world.

Finally, on a special note, I want to share a comment made by my brother's partner, Andrea Mathias, regarding how *Dirty Dancing* positively impacted her sister, Anna Mathias. Anna is thirty-six years old and lives in Budapest, Hungary. "My sister is also a huge fan. I think she continued to go to dance school because of *Dirty Dancing.* She used to have her hair styled like Baby's and even dressed like her!" **Per Anna:** "This enthusiasm for DD happened in my teenage years. During this time, my ideal man was Patrick Swayze. I tried to learn the same choreography presented in this movie while waiting for the day when 'my Patrick' would finally dance this performance with me." **Per Andrea:** "Anna and her husband are great ballroom dancers and they went out a lot to dance when they were dating. Also, he proposed to her at a formal event called the Anna Ball. So her dream came true in a way."

Official *JUMP!* Poster

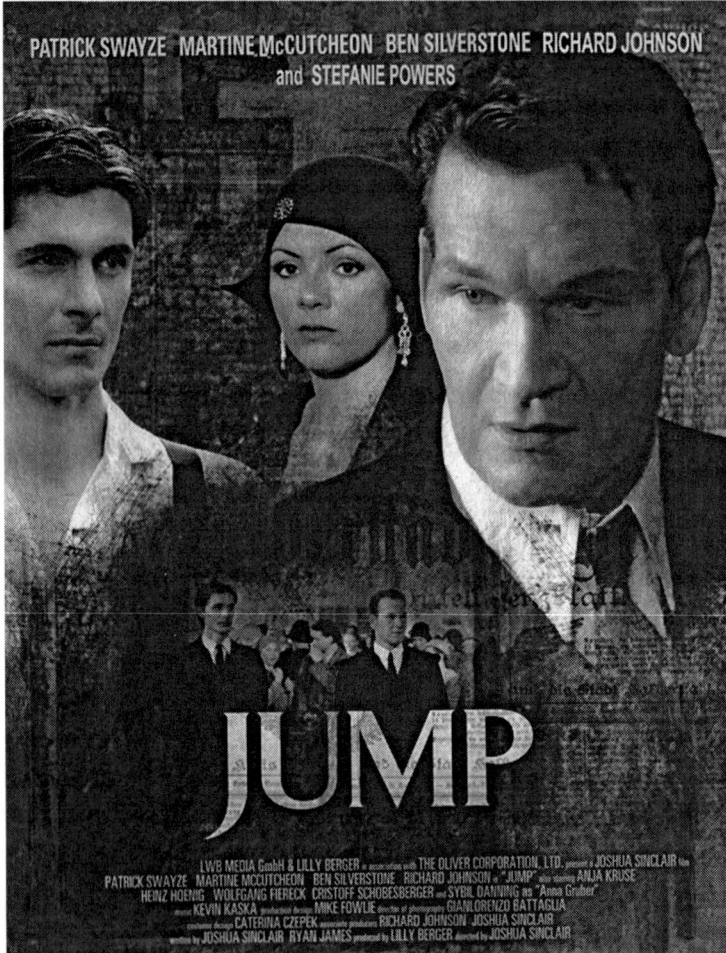

Patrick Swayze was awarded Best International Actor for *Jump!* on May 16, 2009. *Jump!* tells the true story of the acclaimed celebrity photographer Phillippe Halsman; focusing on his murder trial in 1928 in Austria. Patrick is featured as Richard Pressburger, the attorney who helps Phillippe Halsman fight against the rampant anti-Semitism of the time.

Nine

CLOSING

Mr. Patrick Swayze wrote something in the April 2003 issue of *Arts Houston Magazine* regarding the movie *One Last Dance* (written, directed, produced and starred in by Ms. Lisa Niemi, and starred in and produced by Mr. Patrick Swayze) that applies to *Dirty Dancing* just as well:

" . . . the world wants, needs, and demands that a movie change it in some way . . . A movie must make this life more special, or at least bearable, by the realization that someone else feels what we feel, that we are not alone in this world . . . "[15]

Dirty Dancing has definitely—a million times over—changed the world and made it more bearable and special. *Dirty Dancing* is a prime example of how a movie can impact and unite people of all ages, from all over the world, for over twenty years. When you get right down to it, *Dirty Dancing* is about magnificent artistry—storytelling, dancing, acting, music—that showcases humanness, love, integrity, self-discovery, and hope. In today's complex and often stressful world, *Dirty Dancing* provides a place in which the human spirit prevails and triumphs. If only the real world could be more like the *Dirty Dancing* world! I am sure that *Dirty Dancing* will continue to enrich and positively change lives, and bring people together forever.

CANCER ORGANIZATIONS

THE PATRICK SWAYZE PANCREAS CANCER RESEARCH FUND

Stanford Cancer Center

Development Office

2700 Sand Hill Road

Menlo Park

CA 94025

650-234-0651

http://med.stanford.edu/cancer/features/research_news/Patrick_Swayze_Pancreas.html

"Gifts to this fund will support studies to increase our understanding of pancreas cancer and develop new therapies and technologies that can be applied to improving diagnosis, treatment, and prevention. Our goal is to apply a multidisciplinary approach to the study of pancreas cancer and the care of patients afflicted with this disease."

PANCREATIC CANCER ACTION NETWORK

877-272-6226 or 310-725-0025

www.pancan.org

"The Pancreatic Cancer Action Network is a nationwide network of people dedicated to working together to advance research, support patients and create hope for those affected by pancreatic cancer."

STAND UP TO CANCER

888-907-8263

www.standup2cancer.org

"This is where the end of cancer begins: when we unite in one unstoppable movement and Stand Up To Cancer."

ACKNOWLEDGMENTS

I have so much gratitude towards so many people for providing me support, expertise, insight, and heart while I wrote this book. At times, I thought that I would never complete the book, and it seems like there was always somebody there to encourage me to make it to the finish line.

I thank with gratitude Lee Santiwan for her constant "cheerleader" support, feedback, and wisdom.

I thank with gratitude Jackie Horner and Steve Schwartz, the "real" Catskills people for their detailed and meaningful sharing about their lives in the Catskills and how that contributed to the movie.

I thank with gratitude the three people I interviewed that were present during the filming of *Dirty Dancing*:
Buzz Scanland, General Manager at Mountain Lake Hotel, for inviting me to Mountain Lake Hotel and being such a wonderful host and source of information about the movie—including allowing me to use documents from the hotel's records on *Dirty Dancing*; as well as pictures of Mountain Lake Hotel.
Mike Porterfield, Executive Chef at Mountain Lake Hotel, for a fantastic interview and his encouragement and patience with all of my questions.
Gary Wilson, Head of Security at Rumbling Bald Resort, for a wonderful interview.

I thank with gratitude Margaret Howden, President of the Official Patrick

Swayze International Fan Club, for getting the ball rolling by putting my survey online and for her tireless efforts in designing and revising the graphics, and for her computer technical support—as well as amazing emotional support and insight. I also appreciate the access given to me to the club website and magazine to inform people about the book.

I thank with gratitude Crystal Berger for being a gracious first interviewee, providing constant (and I mean constant) feedback, and amazing emotional support and insight throughout the entire writing of the book, and for taking over some of the fan club responsibilities so I would have more time to write the book.

I thank with gratitude Jan Griffith for relieving me from some fan club duties, working on and finalizing the graphics, providing amazing emotional support, and providing me with information on the stage show.

Next I profoundly thank from my heart, the twenty-two fans, who for the most part did not know me and granted me interviews—often revealing very personal information and providing great support in so many ways for the book. Each of you made a very special contribution to the book and I am forever grateful to you:
Elly Ali, Helen Damigou, Clare Gregan, Lelia Bako, Simone Gradl, Angela Grubb, Roy Helton, Becky Williams, Kelly Miner, Barbara Schiebl, Flabia Pennella, Kari Thompson, Crystal L. Berger, Debbie Wallerstein, Cheryl Dubuque, Callie and David Van Kleeck, Mallory Longworth, Barbara Phipps, Evelyn Serian, Doreen Height, and Roberta Teska.

I miss you Evelyn. I greatly appreciate your openness, great sense of humor, and camaraderie that you provided to me.

I have special gratitude to my family and friends for their ongoing support of the book. I thank my mother, Phyllis Friedman, and my father, David Tabashnik for instilling in me at a young age the love of books and for their ongoing support—emotional and financial of the writing of this book. I thank Suzanne Tabashnik (support), Bruce Tabashnik (computer, financial, and editing support), Gabe Tabashnik (support), Andrea Mathias (support, financial), Nedra Kapetansky (especially financial support), Mary Lou Zieve (including financial support), David Tabashnik—my step-brother (photos), Bob Howell, Don Frazier, Jennifer Cantrell, Mark Nocera (computer, photos/images), Mary Kiriazis, Rosemarie Ravenelle, Shirley Penrod, and my work colleagues-you know who you are.

Grandma Lee Tabashnik (who died from pancreatic cancer over twenty years ago)—thanks for your help even from above. Let us hope and work together for a time when there is a cure for all types of cancer, even pancreatic—and then for a time when no type of cancer exists anymore. I salute my other family members who were taken by cancer: Grandma Frieda Zieve, Uncle Mort Zieve, and Aunt Janet Rich. I salute my family members and friends who are cancer survivors.

Special, special thanks to Joshua Sinclair for support and use of the official *Jump!* poster.

Special, special thanks to Larry Jordan and Joan Lowenstein for their expert legal counsel.

Special, special thanks to Nicole Klungle and Sandra Beals for answering questions about editing and book formatting.

Special, special thanks to Ricky Byrd and Jamie Vuignier at The Kobal Collection.

Special, special thanks to Marsha Stevers at Mountain Lake Hotel for assistance with photos and other information.

Special, special thanks to Murray Goldenberg, DJ Rick Pruett, and Warren Bailey for photos.

Special, special thanks to Larry Morando and staff at Outskirts Press.

Finally, I thank Eleanor Bergstein, Emile Ardolino, Jennifer Grey, Jerry Orbach, Cynthia Rhodes, Kenny Ortega, Linda Gottlieb, Miranda Garrison, Kelly Bishop, and all of the people involved in making *Dirty Dancing*—as your creation is held so dear in the hearts of so many people!

BIBLIOGRAPHY

"ABC Gets Another Dance Reality Show." *iCelebZ.com*. June 11, 2009.

"ABC invites Whizz Kid to Dance." *C21 Media 2009*. June 11, 2009.

"ABC puts a twist on 'Dance.'" Michael Schneider. *VARIETY*. June 10, 2009.

"All's Clear, Clean at Mountain Lake." Elizabeth Wilkerson. *The Richmond News Leader*. September 11, 1987.

Barbara Walters Special Interview. ABC. 1988.

"Because You Asked For It: A Dirty Dancing Remake." Neil Miller. *Film School Rejects*. August 19, 2009.

The Big Idea with Donny Deutsch. CNBC. May 25, 2005.

"Biographical Sketch—Jackie Horner." Jackie Horner.

"Body and Soul." Jeannie Park. *People*. August 26, 1991.

"Bringing Dirty Dancing to Life." Meredith Goldstein. *The Boston Globe*. February 1, 2009.

"British Reality TV Series Returns to Mountain Lake." Lindsay Kay. *Roanoke.com*. May 31, 2008.

"The Cast Boogies at 'Dirty' Bash." *USA Today*. August 19, 1987.

"Celebrating 'Dirty Dancing' With Reality TV Show." *ABC 13*. August 26, 2007.

"Choreographer Kenny Ortega's Ode to Disco." Peter Hartlaub. Chronicle Staff Writer. *SFGate.com.* January 16, 2003.

"Codemasters Online Gaming Unveils the Official Dirty Dancing Video Game!" Press release supplied by Games Press. May 29, 2007.

"Coming Soon to Your PC: Dirty Dancing, the Video Game." Susan Arendt. *Wired.* May 29, 2007.

"Complexions Gala!" Sue Tabashnik. *Official Patrick Swayze International Fan Club Magazine.* December 2002.

"Complexions 2004—Detroit." Sue Tabashnik. *Official Patrick Swayze International Fan Club Magazine.* December 2004.

"Dirty Dance Off That Weight." *Health.com.* November 2008.

"Dirty Dancing." Douglas Pratt. *Moviecitygeek.com.* 2004.

"Dirty Dancing." *USA Today.* Susan Wlosczyna. 1997?

"Dirty Dancing: A Legendary Story on National Tour." *Broadway fanclub. com.* The Broadway League. August 2008 Newsletter.

"'Dirty Dancing' at the Hurleyville Museum." *Retrospect.* John Conway. Tower Websites. June 19, 2009.

Dirty Dancing. The Book of The Film. Berndt Schulz. United Kingdom: Ravette Books Limited. 1989.

"'Dirty Dancing' Comes Alive on Stage." Rick Schultz. *The Jewish Journal.* May 20, 2009.

"Dirty Dancing—Dance: 10, Act 3." Nancy Grossman. *Broadwayworld.com.* February 14, 2009.

"Dirty Dancing." The Internet Movie Database. *imdb.com/title/tt0092890.* Including:

"Dirty Dancing." A film review by Sharon Badian. 1987.

"Dirty Dancing." A film review by Ken Perlow. 1987.

"Dirty Dancing: Baby's Out of the Corner." Mike Snider. *USA Today*. April 2007.

"'Dirty Dancing' creator keeps the legend alive." Sid Smith. *Chicago Tribune*. September 28, 2008.

"Dirty Dancing Film Crew Not Afraid To Get Its Hands Dirty." Lindsay Key. *Roanoke Times*. August 18, 2007.

"Dirty Dancing Hits West End." Tom Teodorczuk. *Evening Standard*. February 23, 2006.

"Dirty Dancing is Britain's Top Film." *Contactmusic.co*. May 13, 2009.

"Dirty Dancing is Still Moving People." Jane Sumner. *The Dallas Morning News*. August 31, 1997.

"Dirty Dancing Is Ultimate Movie Medicine." *Contactmusic.com*. January 13, 2006.

"'Dirty Dancing' Makes Stage Debut in London." *Studio Briefing*. October 26, 2006.

"Dirty Dancing Marks 20 Years With Return To Big Screen." Paul Clark. *Citizens-Times.com*. April 30, 2007.

"Dirty Dancing Musical Set for Broadway." *Contactmusic.com*. October 22, 2008.

"Dirty Dancing Prepares for Chicago." *Chicago Sun-Times*. August 5, 2008.

"Dirty Dancing Puts New Life in Resort." *The Buffalo News*. June 26, 1988.

"Dirty Dancing Repackaged for Girls' Night-in." *Contactmusic.com*. August 8, 2008.

"Dirty Dancing Show Having The Time Of My Life." Katherine Tulich. *New Zealand Herald*. April 20, 2006.

"Dirty Dancing. Staff at Mountain Lake Pray for Patrick Swayze." Jean Jadhon. *WDBJ7*. March 8, 2008.

"'Dirty Dancing' star Josef Brown." Colleen Mastony. *Chicago Tribune*. November 19, 2008.

"Dirty Dancing Tangos into Chicago For Pre-Broadway Premiere." Molly Woulf. *Nwitimes.com*. September 28, 2008.

"Dirty Dancing: The Classic Story on Stage." Official website for stage production. *Dirtydancingonstage.com*.

"Dirty Dancing Tickets Sell Fast." *BBC News*. April 13, 2006.

"Dirty Dancing to take the floor again." Ben Child. *Guardian.co.uk*. August 19, 2009.

"Dirty Dancing Tops Most Watched Film Poll for Women." *Daily Mail*. May 6, 2007.

"Dirty Dancing 20th Anniversary." DVD. Lionsgate. 2007.

"Dirty Dancing Ultimate Edition." DVD. Lionsgate. 2003.

"Dirty Dancing Voted Nation's Favourite." *ITV News*. September 12, 2004.

"Dirty Dancing Will Launch U.S. National Tour in September 2008." Andrew Gans. *Playbill*. August 14, 2007.

"Down and 'Dirty.'" ENCORE. *Entertainment Weekly*. August 20, 1999.

"Fans of Dirty Dancing." *Chattanooga News Free Press*. June 27, 1988.

"Film: 'Dirty Dancing' Rocks to an Innocent Beat." Samuel G. Freedman. *The New York Times*. August 16, 1987.

"Film Fans' Dirty Secret: Swayze Tops Their Poll." Fiona MacGregor. *The Scotsman*. July 29, 2005.

"Film Thrills Horner." *Times Herald-Record*. August 18, 1987.

"From Bogart to McGregor: The Top Ten Most Romantic Movie Quotes Ever." Tahira Yaqoob. *Daily Mail.* February 2008.

"Getting Down and Dirty." Charles Leerhsen with Tessa Namuth. *Newsweek.* December 21, 1987.

"Ghost tops best screen kiss poll." *www.digitalspy.co.uk.* July 5, 2008.

"Gottlieb's Grit, Imagination Made Dirty Dancing." Darrell Sifford. *Houston Chronicle.* November 8, 1987.

Growing Up at Grossinger's. Tania Grossinger. New York: Skyhorse Publishing. 2008.

"Hearts Skip A Beat." Deborah Lyon Blumberg. *Home News Tribune Online.* February 26, 2006.

"Hey Baby-we're all Swayze now." Polly Vernon. *The Observer.* September 2006.

It Happened in the Catskills. Myrna Katz Frommer and Harvey Frommer. Albany, New York: Excelsior Editions, State University of New York Press. 2009.

"The Joy of Dirty Dancing." Sue Tabashnik. Official Patrick Swayze International Fan Club Magazine. August 2007.

"Keeping it 'Dirty.'" Kelley Carter. *ChicagoTribune.com.* September 28, 2008.

"Let's Dance for Comic Relief." BBC ONE. *www.bbc.co.uk/letsdance/.*

"Like the Wind." Amy Train. *Modern Arabian Horse.* October/November 2009.

"Lionsgate and National CineMedia's Fathom to Bring Baby out of the Corner and Back on to the Big Screen to Celebrate 20 Years of 'Dirty Dancing.'" Press Release. April 20, 2007.

"Lionsgate Puts Baby in the Corner Again With remake of Dirty Dancing."

Emily Phillips. *Empire: Movie News.* August 19, 2009.

"Live from Nashville Film Festival: 500 Days of Summer, Stacy Widelitz." Joe Leydon. *Cowboys & Indians.* April 16, 2009.

"Lopez and Ex-Husband To Be Dance Rivals." *Contactmusic.com.* May 3, 2006.

"Miranda Garrison talks Dirty Dancing." *www.femalefirst.co.uk/ celebrityinterviews.* September 2, 2008.

"Mountain Lake Hotel." *www.mountainlakehotel.com.*

"Mountain Lake Resort holds a memorial for actor Patrick Swayze." *Virginian Leader.* November 25, 2009.

"Mountain Lake 2008 Newsletter." *www.mountainlakehotel.com.*

"Mountain Lake Resort Hosts Dirty Dancing." Jeremy Byman. *Virginia Film.* March, 1988.

"Mountain Manors." *Washington Post.* October 14, 1988.

"Movie makes her do the mambo, not the munch-o." Neal Rubin. *Detroit Free Press.* January 7, 1988.

"Movie Turns Resort Into Smash Hit." *Road Trip.* January–February 1989.

"National Kissing Day 2008–Patrick Swayze voted top big-screen kisser of all time." *responsesource.com.* July 1, 2008.

"North Carolina: The home of Dirty Dancing where Johnny met Baby." Wendy Gomersall. MailOnline. *Dailymail.co.uk.* January 10, 2010.

"One Last Dance." Patrick Swayze. *Arts Houston Magazine.* April 2003.

The Oprah Winfrey Show: You Tube's Greatest Hits with The Billionaire Founders. Harpo, Inc. November 6, 2007.

"Patrick Swayze Battles Pancreatic Cancer as the World Watches and Prays." Tim King. *Salem-News.com.* May 7, 2009.

"Patrick Swayze on 'Dirty Dancing.'" *Telegraph.co.uk. Guardian News & Media*. September 23, 2006.

"Patrick Swayze Peaceful Warrior." *VENICE Magazine*. Alex Simon. June 2004.

"Patrick Swayze, Song-and-Dance Man." Day to Day. *NPR*. January 12, 2004.

"Patrick Swayze Tops Valentine's Poll*." Contactmusic.com*. February 14, 2009.

"Photos: Swayze and Sweeney Ready To Play in Dolls." *Whatsonstage.com*. Terri Paddock. June 5, 2006.

"Reality TV: Gotta 'Dance?' This show's for you." Madeleine Marr. *Miami Herald*. September 27, 2009.

"Shawshank is feel good favourite." *www.ananova*. February 2008.

"Shrek pair named best movie couple." Beth Hilton. *www.digitalspy.co.uk. February 21, 2008.*

"Singin' In The Rain." Linda Gottlieb. *Premiere*. May 1988.

"Soul Dancing with Swayze." Michelle Garforth. *Renaissance Magazine*. February 2003.

"Stayin' Alive." Mark Shanahan*. The Boston Globe*. Globe Newspaper Company. September 2005.

"Still 'Dancing.'" Rachel B. Levin. *BACKSTAGE.com*. May 8, 2009.

"Supple Limbs in a Sea of Energy." Gia Kourlas. *The New York Times*. November 23, 2009.

"Swayze feels at home in Chicago". Robert K. Elder. *Chicago Tribune*. November 18, 2008.

"Swayze lends support to edgy dance company." *The Oakland Press*. December 2, 2004.

"Swayze nervous over West end bow." *PIPEX.* June 5, 2006.

"This Is It Director Kenny Ortega on Memories of Michael Jackson." Mike Ryan. *Vulture.* October 26, 2009.

"Tickets for East Coast 'Dirty Dancing' Premiere in Boston 10/5." *Broadwayworld.com.* October 1, 2008.

"Time of Her Life Creator of 'Dirty Dancing' brings the 1987 Film Hit to the Stage." Dave Favre. May 8, 2009.

The Time of My Life. Patrick Swayze and Lisa Niemi. New York: Atria Books. 2009.

"The time of their lives: A star of stage and screen." *The Independent.* February 14, 2007.

"There's a secret dancer inside us all." Veronica Lee. *Telegraph.co.uk. Guardian News & Media.* September 23, 2006.

"20 Years of Sexiest Man Alive." *People.* Time Inc. Home Entertainment. 2005.

"20th anniversary screening of Dirty Dancing." Gene Seymour. *Newsday. com.* August 23, 2007.

"UK cinemagoers vote Dirty Dancing as favorite flick." Hadassah Nymark. *Campaignlive.co.uk.* May 13, 2009.

WEBSITES:

International Broadway Database

International Movie Data Base

Official Patrick Swayze International Fan Club

Turner Classic Movies

Wikipedia, The Free Encyclopedia

LaVergne, TN USA
04 December 2010
207258LV00002B/19/P

9 781432 751104